THE BIG VIAGRA JOKEBOOK

No prizes for guessing why he's stuck in the chimney

About the Authors

Mark Leigh and Mike Lepine are both at their sexual peak and have no need whatsoever for Viagra (two ice-lolly sticks and some elastic bands yes, but Viagra, no). In between making love to over 10,000 women between them, they somehow managed to find time to write the following twenty-four books:

Also by Mike Lepine and Mark Leigh

The Complete Revenge Kit
How to Be a Complete Bastard (*with Adrian Edmondson*)
How to Be a Complete Bitch (*with Pamela Stephenson*)
The Book of Revelations
The Naughty '90s
The Return of the Complete Revenge Kit
How to Be a Superhero
The Book of Stupid Lists
How to Be a Real Man (*with Julian Clary*)
The Official Politically Incorrect Handbook
Back to Basics
The Ultimate Revenge Kit
Roy Chubby Brown Unzipped! (*with Roy Chubby Brown*)
The Office Revenge Kit
The Official Politically Incorrect Handbook – Volume 2
Animal Tales (*with Rolf Harris*)
The Extraterrestrial's Guide to *The X-Files*
The Really Rough Holiday Guide
Beastly Behaviour (*with Rolf Harris*)
The Lovers' Revenge Kit
Wannabe a Spice Girl?
The Book of Utterly Ridiculous Stupid Lists
Jeremy Beadle's How to Make Your Own Video Blockbuster
Sports Crazy (*with Des Lynam*)

THE BIG VIAGRA JOKEBOOK

Cartoons by

Gray

MARK LEIGH AND MIKE LEPINE

metro

First published in Great Britain in 1998
by Metro Books (an imprint of Metro
Publishing Limited), 19 Gerrard Street,
London W1V 7LA

British Library Cataloguing in Publication Data. A CIP record of this book is available on request from the British Library.

ISBN 1 900512 64 5

10 9 8 7 6 5 4 3 2 1

Typeset by Wakewing, High Wycombe
Printed in Great Britain by Caledonian,
Glasgow

Acknowledgements

The authors would like to thank the following fine upstanding men (and women) for their contributions and assistance:

Alan Brooke, Steve Choopani, Loretta Cohen, Steve Ellis, Rob Ewen, Gary Fairhead, Anthony Groves, Graham Harper, Graham Hart, Andrea Hatton, Philippa Hatton-Lepine, Sara Howell, Jonathan Landau, Neville Landau, Joe Lawrence, Debbie Leigh, Philip Leigh, Fred Leonard, Steven Markham, Judy Martin, Mark Mathiason, Richard 'Dick' Parker, Ronnie Payne, Robert Pepper, Steve Safran, Julie Smith and John Wright.

The front cover design was done thanks to the inspiration and help of the National Trust Photographic Library.

I've decided to give up sex..
That'll save us a fortune
VIAGRA BILL

A 75-year-old man goes into the doctor's and asks for some Viagra. The doctor says that, before he'll consider prescribing it, he'll need a sperm sample. He gives the elderly man a jar and says come back tomorrow. The next day, the man returns.

'Have you got your sample?' asks the doctor.

'No,' the old man admits. 'I tried everything. I tried with my right hand, then my left. Then both hands. And then my wife tried with her left hand, then her right hand, then with her mouth with her teeth both in and out. We even went round to the lady next door. And she tried it with both hands and her mouth, but it was still no good...'

'You asked the lady next door to help you?' the doctor asks incredulously.

'Yes,' replied the patient. 'She's a strong woman – but even she couldn't get the lid off this goddamn jar.'

What do you call a Viagra user who wins the National Lottery?

– A lucky stiff

'So what happened?' asked the marriage guidance counsellor of the couple before her.

'Well,' the man said, 'it happened after I was prescribed Viagra. Last week I made love to my wife for the first time in about six years and I was so exhausted in the morning that I forgot where I was and left a £20 note on the pillow.'

'That's not so bad,' said the counsellor. You were probably just recalling your carefree, bachelor days before you got married.'

'I know,' the husband replied. 'But how do you explain my wife shouting back, 'You're £20 short!'

An Elizabethan playwright named Will
In bed, was over the hill
They called him the Bard
But he was not very hard
Until Anne Hathaway gave him that pill

A man is nagged mercilessly by his wife until he agrees to go and get some Viagra. He comes home, and she nags him to take a pill immediately. He swallows it and his wife says, 'Now that you're a real man, treat me like a woman!'

So the husband rips off his clothes, flings them to the floor and says, 'Iron these!'

A woman was talking to her friend. 'You look absolutely terrible,' she said. 'You've got bags under your eyes, you're pale and drawn. What happened?'

'I'm exhausted,' the second woman said with a yawn. 'My husband's on Viagra and after we make love, he falls asleep with his penis still inside me.'

'What's so bad about that?' the first woman asked.

'He sleepwalks.'

What do you call an aardvark that can't get hold of some Viagra?

– a Vark.

A man went to his doctor complaining that when he and his wife tried to make love it was a disaster. He couldn't get it up and she was losing patience and was even considering a divorce. He pleaded with the doctor to help save his marriage and, after a quick medical, the doctor prescribed Viagra.

'How long will it take you to get home from here?' the doctor asked.

'About an hour,' the man replied.

'Good. Take one of these now and by the time you get home you'll be sexually aroused and able to satisfy your wife.'

The man popped the pill, thanked the doctor profusely and drove home. By the time he turned into his road he was as stiff as a ramrod and gagging for it.

'Honey, I'm home!' he proclaimed as he burst through the front door, only to discover that his wife had left him a note saying she was out shopping. In a blind panic he phoned the doctor.

'Doctor. You've got to help me!' the man blurted out. 'I've never been so sexually excited but my wife's not going to get home for another two hours. I feel like I'm going to explode!'

'Calm down,' said the doctor. 'Can't you make love to the au pair instead?'

'Doctor,' the man replied, 'when it comes to screwing the au pair, I don't need any pills.'

A Viagra user named Bowen
Had a penis that kept growin' and growin'
It grew to a size
That won him a prize
But it was no good for screwin', just showin'

After many, many years of impotence, a man finally gets his hands on some Viagra and it turns his life around. Within a decade, he goes from being a complete sexual failure to the father of six children. He is so proud of himself that he starts calling his wife 'Mother of Six' – despite the fact that she clearly hates it.

One night they go to a party. The man decides that it's time to go home, and wants to find out if his wife is ready to leave as well. He shouts at the top of his voice, 'Shall we go home, Mother of Six?'

His wife, irritated by her husband's lack of discretion, shouts back, 'Anytime you're ready, Father of Four!'

A man hated his wife so much that he decided to kill her for the insurance money. He confessed this to a doctor friend, who prescribed Viagra.

'But Doc,' the man said with a puzzled look, 'I want to murder her, not screw her.'

'Aha,' the doctor said. 'That's the beauty of this wonder pill. You take three before bedtime and you'll be able to shag her six times a night. By the time the month's out you'll have shagged her to death.'

The man left with a smile on his face and a bottle of Viagra in his pocket. Not only was he going to kill his wife but it would look like a natural death and he'd be enjoying himself into the bargain. The perfect crime!

A month had almost passed when the doctor bumped into his friend in a wheelchair. He looked weak and haggard and was just managing to push himself along.

'Oh my God!' the doctor exclaimed. 'What happened?'

'Don't worry, Doc,' the man reassured him, 'three more days and she'll be dead!'

That was quick – let's take it outside for some fresh air

Newsflash!

Doctors have now combined Viagra with a hair restorer. It's for real boneheads!

An old man staggered through the door of a whore house in Nevada, holding on to his Zimmer frame for dear life. The buxom receptionist stared at him and exclaimed, 'Hey, old-timer, you must be in the wrong place. This here's the world-famous Pussy Galore Ranch.'

'I know,' replied the old man, his voice quivering. 'Is it true that you have thirty willing girls who'll service me?'

'That's right,' the receptionist replied. 'Thirty young, beautiful girls ready, willing and able – which is more than I can say for you. Tell me, Pop: how old are you?'

'Ninety-six,' the man proudly boasted. 'But I'm taking Viagra.'

'Viagra or not, at ninety-six, you've had it!'

'Oh,' said the old man sadly, as his shaking fingers took out his wallet. 'How much do I owe you?'

10 other new drugs Pfizer have developed following the success of Viagra

1. *Flyagra* – for men who want to join the 'Mile High Club'
2. *Cryagra* – for men who want to be that little bit more sensitive in bed
3. *Myagra* – for men who want a little 'quality time' alone
4. *Lieagra* – for men who didn't come home last night. (Available in Regular, Grand Jury, and Presidential Strength versions.)
5. *Piagra* – for impotent mathematicians
6. *Biagra* – for men who swing both ways
7. *Tieagra* – keeps your neckwear straight
8. *Guyagra* – for men who want to get it up like a rocket on 5 November
9. *Spyagra* – for men who want to turn 007 into 012
10. *Fryagra* – for men who work in fish and chip shops who want their wives to lie back and say 'fillet'.

Which cartoon character desperately needs some Viagra?

– Droopy.

No matter how hard he tried, George couldn't save any of his wages. Then one day he hit upon a scheme – a rather unique way to put some money aside each week. He was taking Viagra and told his wife Sue that since he was pumped full of sexual energy, each time he made love to her, he would put a pound coin in a piggy bank. Since he was making love to his wife at least once a night every night of the week, the money would soon mount up.

George kept his promise and a few weeks later he smashed open the piggy bank. It was full of pound coins but also loads of fivers, ten pound notes, even a few twenties.

'Sue,' George asked his wife, 'where did you get all that money? Every time I screwed you I only gave you a pound!'

'So what?' Sue replied indignantly. 'Do you think everyone is as mean as you?'

Joe went to stay with a friend who lived on a farm and was fascinated by the modern milking machine. He watched his friend attach a rubber tube to the udders of a cow and switch it on. The machine clicked and whirred and within a few seconds it was gently sucking the milk into a large churn.

That evening Joe couldn't wait and popped a Viagra pill. An hour later he crept out of his room into the milking shed. By the time he arrived, he had a massive hard-on which he inserted into the end of the milking machine and switched it on just to see how it felt.

Two hours later, awoken by the sound of the milking machine, his friend found Joe writhing in agony on the barn floor, moaning and groaning, his eyes glazed over. 'For God's sake,' he begged, 'turn it off! Turn that damn milking machine off!'

'What on earth are you playing at?' his friend asked in amazement.

'I took Viagra then stuck my dick in your bloody machine to see what it was like. This is the sixtieth time I've come and I can't turn it off!' Joe explained.

His friend could only shrug his shoulders. 'I can't turn it off either.'

'What do you mean?' Joe asked, coming for the sixty-first time.

His friend explained, 'It's automatic. But don't worry, the thing's only set for forty pints.'

A Viagra user called Spence
Had an erection that was immense
When it was hard
He charged girls £1 for a yard
And often made sixty-six pence

An elderly man goes into the confession booth and says to the priest, 'Father, I'm eighty-seven years old, married, have four kids and 11 grandchildren. I started taking this new Viagra pill, and last night I had an affair and made love to two 18-year-old twins. I had both of them, three times.'

The priest can't believe it and asks, 'Well, my son, when was the last time you were in confession?'

'Never Father, I'm Jewish,' replies the old man.

'So then, why are you telling me?' asks the astonished priest.

'I'm telling everybody!'

What do you call a skinhead that uses Viagra?

– A real hard nut

A Viagra user called Durand
Had a dick that was ever so grand
Girls gasped at its size
And tears soon filled their eyes
As they watched it expand and expand

Newsflash!

Doctors today released a Viagra patient from hospital after an unforeseen side-effect turned him into a sofa. His condition is described as 'comfortable'.

What happened when the Brigadier-General used Viagra toothpaste?

– He got a stiff upper lip.

Not many people know this, but Viagra was originally invented to improve your golf game and doctors were concerned that increased sexual excitement and an uncontrollable libido might be an unwanted side-effect. One of the early test subjects was a keen amateur golfer. They gave him the pills, sent him away and re-interviewed him after 30 days. 'How was it?' the boffins asked him.

'It worked!' said the golfer. 'It really did! I'm now the club champion!'

'Yes, but what about your sex life?' the boffins asked, afraid of the answer.

'It's OK,' answered the golfer. 'I've had sex six or seven times in the past month.'

Everyone in the lab gave a sigh of relief. That was within the acceptable boundaries.

'Thank goodness it's that low,' one of the boffins said.

'Low?' said the golfer. 'Well I don't think it's bad at all for a Catholic priest in a small parish.'

Shall we go to bed or do you want to stay up all night?
Yes

15 things not to say if you want your GP to prescribe you Viagra

1. I need it – my wife's even uglier than yours.
2. I'm 102 tomorrow, you know…
3, Give me a prescription and I'll be back in an hour to slip you one, Doc…
4. Ughhh! What was that mysterious constricting twinge in my chest just then?
5. I've got to have some; the Jamboree starts tomorrow…
6. It's no fun flashing women with a limp one…
7. I've just bought a very flirty chicken.
8. I've just bought a very flirty oven-ready chicken.
9. I know all you doctors are on the take. Here's 50p. Get me a couple of bottles…
10. Of course, I don't really need it, I just want you to examine my genitals.
11. Tell you what, I'll sell them for a fiver a pop and we'll split the proceeds.
12. I'm seeing your wife tonight.
13. I'm seeing your daughter tonight.
14. I'm seeing your wife and daughter tonight.
15. I'm seeing your son tonight.

What do you get if you stick a Viagra tablet in each ear?

– Hard of hearing

A White House adviser walked into the daily briefing meeting a little late and noticed that everyone had a worried look on their faces. The President hadn't arrived yet so he asked what was wrong.

'Well, we've heard some bad news and some even worse news,' said one of the Chiefs of Staff. 'Iraq has detonated some atomic weapons at an underground test site. Libya has done the same. And Israel has warned them both that this could lead to a regional war that might go nuclear!'

'Oh my God!' the anxious adviser exclaimed. 'What could be worse than that?'

'Well. Bill just got hold of some Viagra.'

A Viagra user from Devizes
Has a penis of two different sizes
When you observe it at ease
It hangs down to his knees
God knows what it's like when it rises

An impotent man was so pleased with the effect of Viagra that he ran out of his house, drove to the red-light district and picked up the first prostitute he could find, just to try it out. A week later he was at the doctor's, being told that he had a bad case of VD.

Enraged, he stormed out of the surgery, got in his car and screeched to a halt right at the corner where the same hooker was plying her trade. He shouted out the window, 'You f*cking bitch! You gave me VD!'

'That's bullshit!' replied the hooker. 'I did not give you the clap. You bought it!'

The crusty old chairman of a large corporation was amazed at how Viagra had improved his libido. Tonight was the night he planned to seduce his pretty young secretary, starting off by taking her to dinner at the Savoy. After a few pre-dinner cocktails the secretary ordered the finest pâté de foie gras, the best filet mignon, two desserts from the trolley – not forgetting vintage Dom Perignon to wash the meal down.

As he paid the £260 bill the old chairman looked at his secretary and asked in amazement, 'Does your mother feed you like this?'

'No,' replied the secretary, wiping the last dessert crumbs from her full red lips, 'but my mother's not planning to shag me, either!'

Newsflash!

Doctors today released a Viagra patient from hospital after an unforeseen side-effect made one of his legs drop off. His condition is described as 'stable'.

A Viagra user named Pete
Shagged his wife in their car on the street
Two jerks plus a spasm
Produced an orgasm
That stuck them both fast to the seat

What happens if you mix Viagra and iron pills?

– You still get an erection but it always points north

Despite taking Viagra, George was a disappointment to his girlfriend the first time they went to bed. No matter how much he tried, he couldn't satisfy her. Sensing that she was as frustrated as he was, George asked what was wrong.

'That's easy,' the girl replied. 'Your organ's nowhere near big enough.'

'Well that's partly your fault,' Bill replied. 'I had no idea I'd be playing in a cathedral!'

HOTEL

Two elderly men go on a sex holiday to Thailand. They head straight for a local massage parlour, pick up some prostitutes and then – disaster – neither can get it up.

'One of us will have to find a chemist and get some Viagra,' one suggests. 'Only what's Thai for Viagra?'

'It doesn't matter,' says the other. 'Just go inside, slap your limp penis down on the counter, point to it. Offer the chemist a tenner. He'll understand.'

So the man goes off but soon returns, looking very miserable.

'Did you get the Viagra?' his friend asks.

'No,' his friend admits.

'Well why not? Did you do what I told you to do?'

'Yes,' says the first man. 'I went inside. I put a tenner on the counter. I put my knob on the counter. He put his on the counter. It was bigger than mine. Then he takes my tenner.'

Why should you put Viagra in your car's petrol tank?

– It helps the big end to last longer.

Louise was in bed with her husband, waiting for the effects of his Viagra pill to kick in. Suddenly his dick started growing, and growing, and growing. When she saw the eventual size of his penis, Louise leapt out of bed and ran into the kid's room, returning a few seconds later.

'What are you doing?' her husband enquired.

'Just getting a crayon,' she told him. 'Well, you've got to draw the line somewhere.'

A doddery old man went into a brothel and asked to see the madam. She was surprised to see a man of his advanced years at her establishment. 'What can I do for you, sir?' she asked.

'I've just taken Viagra and I need a girl. Now,' the old man replied. 'What will it cost me?'

'My standard charge is £250,' the madam replied, hoping to discourage him.

'You're putting me on!,' he exclaimed in amazement.

'In that case, that will be an extra £40,' said the madam.

If a man's stiff for more than three minutes it's either because he's on Viagra – or he's dead.

Newsflash!

Rumours are rife in Washington that Monica Lewinsky has been taking Viagra. She figures that if she can get an erection she might have a go at Hillary too.

A Viagra user from Maine
Had a dick as stiff as a cane
He attached cloth and some spokes
Extended it with a stroke
And kept himself dry from the rain

Three women were bragging about their husbands.

The first said, 'My husband is special. He bought me a new BMW for my birthday.'

The second woman said, 'My husband is also special. For our anniversary he bought me a mink coat and a pair of one carat diamond earrings.'

The third woman said, 'Well, my husband isn't as rich as both your husbands but he's also special. He takes Viagra and when he has an erection, his penis is so long that ten birds can stand on it side by side.'

The first two women were aghast. There was a long silence before the first one piped up. 'Actually,' she said, 'I lied about my husband. He didn't really buy me a new BMW, he bought me an old Volkswagen Beetle.'

'I'm afraid I also told a fib,' the second lady admitted. 'My husband didn't really buy me a mink coat or diamond earrings. He bought me a new pair of shoes.' Both women turned to the third in anticipation.

'All right! All right!' she said. 'I exaggerated a little as well. When I said that after taking Viagra my husband can get ten birds standing side by side along his penis, I was lying. The tenth bird can only stand on one leg.'

One day a man went to a small chemist shop and asked the little old lady serving behind the counter if he could speak with the resident pharmacist.

'I am the pharmacist,' she told him.

'Oh, in that case, it doesn't matter,' he replied and started to leave.

'Young man,' the old lady said to him, 'My sister and I have been running this shop for fifty years and there is nothing we haven't heard or seen, so please tell us your problem.'

'Well,' the man said reluctantly, 'I have trouble with erections.'

'Well look, if you've come here to ask about Viagra, I'm afraid we can't sell it over the counter,' says the little old lady. 'You'll have to see your doctor.'

'No,' says the man, 'I don't actually need it, you see. My problem is that once I get an erection my penis stays hard for about eight hours. No matter how many times I have sex, or how many times I masturbate, it just won't go down. It's very, very uncomfortable. What can you give me for it?'

'I see,' said the pharmacist. 'Look, wait here a moment. I'll have to go in the back and talk to my sister,' she informed him.

About five minutes later she came back. 'Young man, I have consulted with my sister and the best we can give you is £100 a week and a one-third interest in the shop.'

Does it ever occur to you I may resent being treated as a sex-object?
Frankly, no

15 things you *hope* your GP will never say before he writes you a prescription

1. Beg!
2. It's God's will you're impotent and we should respect that.
3. Sorry, I've just prescribed myself the last 50,000 bottles in the country. Hahahahaha!
4. You don't need Viagra. You need Lourdes…
5. So you think you're impotent? Let's just quickly try the old 'blow job' test…
6. You don't want Viagra. What you want is extreme penile acupuncture with a rusty nail
7. Yes, you can have Viagra. Ha! April Fool!
8. Yes, you can have Viagra. Oh dear, my pen's run out so I can't write your prescription…
9. With a penis your size, it's all a bit academic anyway…
10. Thank you! That's the best laugh I've had in ages!
11. I'm just going to call your best mate for a second opinion.
12. If you just acknowledge you're gay, it'll cure itself…
13. On one condition. That you try your first pill on me.
14. I'll prescribe you Viagra – but you'll have to give up sex.
15. Contamination Level D! Contamination Level D! Seal the surgery!

A husband and his wife go to see their GP to complain about the Viagra the husband has been prescribed.

'Isn't it working?' asks the doctor.

'Oh yes,' says the man. 'It works all right. I didn't used to be bothered about sex much before. Neither did the wife. Now I can't get enough.'

'So what seems to be the problem? Are you suffering from any side-effects?' continues the doctor.

'I'm not, it's the wife,' the husband explains.

'Yes,' his wife pipes up. 'I've got bad knee pains something chronic.'

'Well, that can't be the Viagra,' says the doctor, baffled. 'It must be something you're doing to your knees. Can you think of what it might be?'

'Well,' she says a little sheepishly, 'my husband and I have sex doggy-style on the floor every night.'

'That's got to be it,' said the doctor. 'There are plenty of other positions and ways to have sex, you know.'

'Not if you're going to watch TV there ain't,' she replies.

What do you get when you dissolve Viagra in whisky?

– A touch of the hard stuff

A Viagra user named Spock
Was famed for his elongated cock
It hung like a tail
Until it touched a live rail
And shrivelled with a 5,000 volt shock

Newsflash!

Pfizer have invented a pill for women in answer to Viagra. One hour after taking it she gets a headache that last for three hours.

'I don't really blame the Viagra,' said an elderly lady at her husband's funeral. 'After all, it made a new man of poor old Ernie. We rediscovered sex for the first time in 30 years and, every Sunday morning, we'd make love to the rhythm of the church bells. And if that bloody fire engine hadn't driven by, he'd still be alive today!'

Two men worked in an office with a particularly dominating boss. They felt completely emasculated by him, and their sex lives began to suffer and then disappeared altogether. One Monday morning, one of the men came in with a huge smile on his face and told the other, 'John, I've found the solution. I just take some Viagra and go home and make passionate love to my wife. After that, the world feels good again. Here,' he slipped John a Viagra pill, 'You try it!'

'OK,' said John. He knocked back the pill and rushed out of the office. About three hours later, he sneaked in again.

'Hey,' said his friend, 'you look so much better! Did you do what I told you? Was I right?'

'You certainly were,' said John, 'and by the way, you've got a really nice house.'

50 songs for Viagra users

1. 'Hard Day's Night' – Beatles
2. 'All Night Long' – Lionel Richie
3. 'Baggy Trousers' – Madness
4. 'Theme From *Shaft*' – Isaac Hayes
5. 'More and More' – Andy Williams
6. 'Everything She Wants' – Wham
7. 'From New York to LA' – Patsy Gallant
8. 'Endless Love' – Diana Ross and Lionel Richie
9. 'All the Man that I Need' – Whitney Houston
10. 'Eight Miles High' – Byrds
11. 'How Deep Is Your Love?' – Bee Gees
12. 'All Around My Hat' – Steeleye Span
13. 'Boys Keep Swinging' – David Bowie
14. 'All Day and All of the Night' – Kinks
15. 'In Too Deep' – Genesis
16. 'Everybody Hurts' – REM
17. 'Five Miles Out' – Mike Oldfield
18. 'Rock Around the Clock' – Bill Haley and the Comets
19. 'Ain't Complaining' – Status Quo
20 'Deep and Wide and Tall' – Aztec Camera
21. 'How Long?' – Ace
22. 'Big in Japan' – Alphaville
23. 'Ain't No Mountain High Enough' – Diana Ross
24. 'The Bangin' Man' – Slade
25. 'Love Machine' – Miracles

26. 'All of Me' – Sabrina
27. 'Hurt So Good' – Susan Cadogan
28. 'If It Don't Fit, Don't Force It' – Kelly Patterson
29. 'All the Way from Memphis' – Mott the Hoople
30. 'Love Lifts Us Up Where We Belong' – Jennifer Warnes and Joe Cocker
31. 'Be Stiff' – Devo
32. 'Best Thing that Ever Happened to Me' – Gladys Knight and the Pips
33. 'Don't Love Me Too Hard' – The Nolans
34. 'I am a Rock' – Paul Simon
35. 'Suddenly' – Billy Ocean
36. 'Can't Buy Me Love' (now you can) – Beatles
37. 'Do That to Me One More Time' – Captain and Tenille
38. 'Everlasting Love' – Bee Gees
39. 'Longer' – Dan Fogelberg
40. 'No Ordinary Love' – Sade
41. 'Help Me Make It Through the Night' – John Holt
42. 'Love Takes Time' (about an hour wait – according to Pfizer) – Mariah Carey
43. 'The Power of Love' – Celine Dion
44. 'The Things We Do For Love' – 10CC
45. 'Keep On Loving You' – REO Speedwagon
46. 'Have You Never Been Mellow' – Kris Kristofferson

47. 'Girls Just Want to Have Fun' – Cindy Lauper
48. 'The Only Way Is Up' – Yazz
49. 'When I'm 64' – Beatles
50. 'Bad Medicine' – Bon Jovi

A man walks into a late-night chemist and gets a prescription for Viagra. As soon as he has paid for it, he starts laughing and walks out. The next month, the same performance, with the man walking out laughing fit to bust. The chemist thinks this is very odd and, the next month, he tells his assistant that, when the man returns, to follow him.

Sure enough, the man walks into the chemist's, repeating his actions once more. The assistant duly follows. Half an hour later, he returns.

'So did you follow him?' the manager asks.

'I did.'

'And...where did he go?'

'Over to your house...'

Your wife says
You're impotent
Yeah? What does
my girlfriend say?

What happens when you take too much Viagra?

– When they bury you, the cemetery only needs one stick to make the cross.

After Viagra was discovered, the same group of scientists thought they'd try it out on women. To their amazement they found that it also made them aroused, but that this heightened state of horniness lasted far, far longer than with men. Some of the women found they felt horny for weeks at a time and this was extremely uncomfortable for them.

The scientists then set about trying to discover a simple foodstuff that they could take which would immediately put an end to this limitless sexual desire. They succeeded; it's called 'wedding cake'.

Why should unmarried men without girlfriends be given Viagra too?

– So that they can still have sex with someone they love.

Newsflash!

The makers of Viagra have announced plans to make the drug in wafer form. The Vatican has given its approval, commenting that its use at Communion will give a whole new meaning to 'thy rod and thy staff, they comfort me...'

After twenty years as nothing more than a useless, floppy appendage, this man's penis has been brought back to life again. Revitalized and invigorated, he feels huge and manly once more. In fact, he can't stop himself from showing it to his wife.

A few weeks later, this man and his wife are at the zoo and the man can't resist flashing the elephant with his newly invigorated member, 'Get a load of this, Jumbo!' he shouts.

'Yeah, it's cute,' replies the elephant, 'but can it pick up peanuts?'

A man goes into a doctor's surgery. The receptionist asks him what's wrong and he says, 'I'm a Viagra patient and want to see the doctor about my cock.'

The receptionist reprimands him and says, 'Please! There are women and children in the waiting room.' She then whispers to him, 'If you want to describe that part of your anatomy, just say 'ear' and I'll know what you're talking about.'

The man apologizes, goes out then comes back in.

'And what seems to be the matter, sir?' the receptionist asks.

'I've got a problem with my ear,' the man says.

'That's much better!' smiles the receptionist.

'Yes,' says the man. 'It hurts when I piss.'

A Viagra user down in Lahore
Had a penis that reached down to the floor
He had to carry the thing
In a surgical sling
To stop it from getting red raw

5 Shakespeare plays that might have been about Viagra

1. *King John*
2. *As You Like It*
3. *All's Well that Ends Well*
4. *Twelfth Night*
5. *Measure For Measure*

A constable based at Clapham Junction
Had a penis that had long ceased to function
'Get Viagra,' his wife nagged
But she didn't get shagged –
He just satisfied her with his truncheon

What's the difference between Niagra and Viagra?

– Niagra Falls

A 90-year-old man is sitting on a park bench, sobbing, when a young man walks by and asks him what's wrong. Through his tears the old man answers, 'I'm in love with a 25-year-old woman who's moved in with me.'

'What on earth's wrong with that?' asks the young man.

Between his sobs and sniffles, the older man answers, 'You don't understand. Since the doctor gave me Viagra, I can make love like a machine. Every morning before she leaves my house to go to work, we make love... At lunchtime she comes home and we make love again, and then she makes my favourite meal. In the afternoon when she gets a break, she rushes home and gives me oral sex, the best an old man could want. And then, at supper time, and all night long, we make love.'

He breaks down, no longer able to speak. The young man puts his arm around him. 'I don't understand. It sounds wonderful! Why are you crying?'

The old man bawls through his tears, 'I forgot where I live!'

Newsflash!

The Society of Undertakers are finding Viagra is very disrupting to their business. Last week eight men died after taking it and they still can't close the coffins.

A man goes into Boots and asks the pharmacist, 'Do you sell Viagra?'

The pharmacist says 'Yes' and the man asks, 'Well can I get it over the counter?'

To which the pharmacist replies, 'Well maybe, but you'll have to take three or four of them first…'

A Viagra user from Hong Kong
Possessed quite a remarkable dong
When he was tensing
He could use it for fencing
And even for sounding a gong

A middle-aged couple visit the doctor together to try and find a cure for the husband's impotence. They've heard all about the new wonder drug Viagra but the doctor is religious and would rather trust in God first before resorting to medicine.

The couple find this attitude a bit strange but are willing to give it a go.

The doctor says to the couple, 'I want you to both pray for the impotence to be gone, but before that, you sir, you put your right hand in the air and place your left hand on the afflicted area.'

The man dutifully places his right hand in the air and his left hand on his crotch but just as he's about to pray his wife pipes up, 'Darling, he said he could heal the sick, not raise the dead!'

Doctors have been instructed to describe the group of men who die from complications after taking Viagra as 'the deceased', not 'a bunch of stiffs'.

Are you on the pill?

While carrying out a vasectomy on an anaesthetized man, the doctor slipped and cut off one of the man's balls. To avoid a huge malpractice suit, he decides to replace the missing ball with an onion. Then, to ensure that the man didn't suspect anything, he suggests he try 'some free Viagra samples'.

Several weeks later, the patient returned for a check up. 'How's your sex life?' the doctor asked.

'Pretty good,' the man said, to the doctor's relief. But then he added, 'I've had some strange side-effects from that Viagra stuff you gave me.'

'Oh, like what?'

'Well, every time I piss, my eyes water. When my wife gives me a blow job she gets heartburn. And every time I pass a hamburger stand, I get a hard-on!'

A Viagra user named Paul
Had quite an extraordinary tool
Because of his dick
And the way that he kicked
It was said he was hung like a mule

Two old-timers have a whale of a time when they're both prescribed Viagra. They can't imagine life without it. In fact, they start to fret that, when they die and go to heaven, there won't be any Viagra there. So they make a pact – the first one to die and make it to heaven will come back and let the other know if there is, in fact, Viagra in heaven.

A few months later, one of the old men suffers a massive heart attack while making love to his wife for the fourth time that night. The next day, the other man is sitting in the park, when he feels a light tap on his shoulder. He turns round to see the ghost of his friend sitting beside him.

'So,' he says, 'don't keep me in suspense. Is there Viagra in heaven?'

'Well,' says the ghost, 'I've got some good news and some bad news. The good news is, yes they do prescribe Viagra in heaven.'

'And what's the bad news?' asks his friend.

'Your prescription will be ready to pick up next Tuesday…'

A woman visited her doctor, a family friend, to confide that she thought her husband was having an affair. Her suspicions were aroused by the fact that their sex life was now virtually non-existent whereas when they'd got married a few years ago, they used to make love all the time.

The doctor listened compassionately and told her not to worry. Her suspicions were probably groundless and the lack of interest in sex was probably a result of his age – after all, he was fifteen years older than her. However, to allay her fears he agreed to prescribe Viagra.

'Next time you're having dinner together slip one of these in his drink when he's not looking. I think you'll find they have the desired effect.'

With that he gave her a bottle of Viagra and sent her on her way, asking her to come back in a week's time and let him know how she got on.

In less than a week the woman was back in his office, looking radiant and very fulfilled.

'You look wonderful, my dear!' the doctor commented. 'Did the pills work?'

'Oh yes!' she replied, beaming. 'I slipped one of them in his drink when he wasn't looking, like you said and in less than an hour he was staring at me with lust in his eyes! Without any words being spoken he ripped off his trousers and pants and before I could stop him he'd flung the meal on to the floor and we made mad, passionate love on the table, there and then!

'Fantastic!' the doctor exclaimed. 'I knew the pills would work!'

'Oh it was wonderful!,' the woman added. 'There's just one thing, though.'

'And what's that?' asked the doctor

'I don't think we'll be able to show our faces in Pizzaland ever again.'

How do you find an old man on Viagra in the dark?

– Actually, it's quite hard.

A Viagra user from Harrow
Had a penis the size of a marrow
He could only get round
And move about town
By pushing it along in a barrow

A young man goes into a chemist to buy condoms. The pharmacist says the condoms come in packs of 3, 9 or 12 and asks which the young man wants.

'Well,' he said, 'I've been seeing this old slapper for a while and between you and me, she's gagging for it. I want the condoms because I think tonight's 'the' night. I've been invited round to dinner with her parents and then we're going out. I'm going to get her drunk as a skunk, then it's back to my place to give her one. Trouble is though, she's a bit of an old barker, know what I mean. So in case I need a bit of help to give the dog a bone, what about me slipping you a tenner and you slipping me a couple of Viagras on the QT, nudge, nudge, wink, wink!'

The chemist finds this customer particularly odious, turns his request for Viagra down flat but sells him a packet of three.

Later that evening, the young man is sitting down to dinner with his girlfriend and her parents. Just before they eat he asks her father if he may be permitted to say grace, and they agree.

He begins the prayer, but continues praying for several minutes. The girl leans over and whispers, 'You never told me that you were such a religious person.'

He leans over to her and says, 'You never told me that your dad was a chemist!'

The doctor was puzzled by the Viagra patient standing naked before him. He was aware of all the drug's side-effects that had been reported in the medical journals but he hadn't seen anything like this before – three red rings at the base of the man's penis.

He gave the man a course of antibiotics but the red marks were still there. Over the next few weeks he tried injections, creams, lotions, ointments but still they didn't go away. Eventually the man came back to the surgery, took his trousers and pants down and showed the doctor that the rings had all gone.

'What on earth did you use to get rid of them?' asked the astonished doctor.

'Oh it was nothing special,' replied the man sheepishly, 'just lipstick remover.'

Newsflash!

Reports are coming in that a Viagra delivery truck has been hijacked. The police are looking for four hardened criminals.

A man was feeling particularly run down so he went to his GP for a check-up.

He was dumbstruck when the examination revealed that he was suffering from an incurable disease which meant he only had 24 hours to live.

'Normally,' said the doctor, 'I wouldn't ever do this, but since you've only got 24 hours ahead of you I'm going to give you some Viagra so that at least you can really enjoy what little time you have left.'

The man went home to tell his wife and they both had a long cry over the situation. He told her about the Viagra, took a pill, and they went upstairs to make love, so that his last hours on earth would be enjoyable.

The Viagra had the desired effect and they had fabulous sex. Four hours later they were lying in bed and he turned to her again, and said, 'You know I only have 20 hours to live, do you think we could do it again?'

Again she responded very sympathetically and they made love, as passionately as before.

Another eight hours passed, and the wife was asleep from exhaustion. Her husband tapped her on the shoulder to wake her up and asked her again, 'You know dear, I only have 12 more hours left, how about again for old time's sake?'

By this time she was getting a little annoyed, but reluctantly agreed.

After they finished, she went back to sleep and four hours later, he woke her up again for yet more sex, saying, 'Darling, I hate to keep bothering you but you know I only have eight hours left before I die, can we do it one more time?'

This time his wife turned to him and said with a grimace, 'Look. You know I love you but I've got to get up in the morning. You don't!!!'

A Viagra user from Peking
Complained at his ten inch-long-thing
For all the girls in China
Had very small vaginas
No bigger than the width of his ring

Why did the man dissolve Viagra in water?

– He wanted a stiff drink.

25 tell–tale signs that your grandpa is using Viagra

1. One of the old ladies in his retirement home is found handcuffed to her Zimmer frame.
2. Now you hear two things creaking at night – his joints and his bed.
3. He no longer complains about lumbago or rheumatoid arthritis, just carpet burns.
4. His 'companion' is a 19-year-old lingerie model.
5. His electronically adjustable orthopaedic bed is set for 'doggy-style'.
6. You notice a pubic hair caught in his dentures.
7. A '69' is now what he indulges in, not his age 20 years ago.
8. He blew last week's pension on a party pack assortment of flavoured condoms instead of fags, milk stout and a copy of *Sporting Life*.
9. He treats Saga Holidays like a 'Club 65–80'.
10. He's more concerned about getting VD than Alzheimer's disease.
11. Your granny's moved in with you.
12. He's smiling again.
13. He's finally having something done about the boils.
14. You've never known him take an interest in clean underwear before.
15. He's started smelling of Lynx instead of week-old wee.

16. He's stopped trying to find a 'Mercy Doctor'…
17. He's painted 'Love Machine' on the side of his invalid carriage.
18. He's 89, but he looks 110.
19. Even the cat isn't safe anymore…
20. What you assumed were bed sores are actually love bites.
21. He's stalking Thora Hird.
22. He's stopped lying there in a puddle of his own urine, moaning, 'kill me'...
23. He used to say 'You're as old as you feel.' Now he says, 'You're as old as the woman you feel'...
24. Instead of yakking on and on about the Great War, he yaks on and on about this Great Whore.
25. He put his back out trying to open his bottle of pills.

Why is the funeral industry happy about deaths from Viagra?

– There's an upswing in business caused by lots of new stiffs

Two 70-year-old women were chatting about their sex lives. The first proudly said, 'My husband's on Viagra. He pops a pill and an hour later he's taking me from behind, doggy-style.'

'You don't know how lucky you are,' replied the second old woman. 'My husband can only do it coyote-style. He can't get it up; all he does is lie beside the hole and howl.'

Why do Viagra users name their penises?

– They want to be on a first-name basis with the person who makes all their decisions.

Newsflash!

Gun-wielding thieves held up a North London pharmacy and stole 450 Viagra pills. The suspects are reported to be armed, dangerous and wearing extremely baggy trousers.

I still like it - if only I could remember what it is..

A Native American goes to see a doctor at a big city hospital. 'Me..um...need heap plenty Viagra White Man medicine,' he says.

'Why, what's the problem?' the doctor asks.

'Whole Souix tribe depend on my totem pole to tell time. No get it up, miss TV, bars close, whole tribe disaster!'

'Your tribe tells the time using your erect penis?' the doctor asks. 'I don't believe it. Show me!'

He gives the Native American a Viagra tablet and an hour later takes him outside into the hospital grounds. 'So, what time is it?' The Native American strips off, lies down with his erection in the air and says, '12.30pm'.

The doctor looks at his watch and says, 'That's right. Unbelievable!'

A few hours later, he tries again. The Native American lies down, penis in the air and says, 'Ugg...3pm', and he's right.

So the doctor takes him back inside, gives him a prescription and then sees his other patients. When he comes out of his surgery he is astounded to see the Native American sitting in the waiting room, masturbating furiously.

'Now what the hell are you doing?' he asks.

The Native American says, 'Winding clock.'

What did the doctor say to his patient who discovered he was allergic to Viagra?

– No hard feelings

The day after a man had been prescribed Viagra he returned to the surgery and asked the doctor to examine his penis. The man pulled down his trousers and pants to reveal a massive erection, the likes of which the doctor had never seen. His member stood proudly to attention at about 60 degrees, as hard as a rock. The doctor squeezed it, poked it and prodded it. He listened to it with his stethoscope, looked closely at it with a magnifying glass and even put his ear to it. Eventually he sat back and scratched his head.

'I can't find a thing wrong with it,' said the puzzled doctor.

'I know,' the man said beaming, 'it's brilliant, isn't it?'

Newsflash!

A man was rushed to hospital today after getting a Viagra tablet stuck in his throat. Fortunately, he suffered from nothing more serious than a stiff neck.

The Viagra patient called his lawyer. 'I want to sue the makers of Viagra and I want to divorce my wife!' he said angrily.

'Why, what's the problem?' his lawyer asked.

'Well, first of all the Viagra I've been taking didn't work. And because of that, my wife says I'm crap in bed.'

'You'll lose both cases,' the lawyer advised. 'Firstly, there's no guarantee with Viagra. And secondly, you can't divorce your wife just because she says you're a lousy lover,' he added.

'No,' the man admitted, 'but I'm divorcing her because she knows the difference!'

Viagra had rejuvenated a 90-year-old man's sex life and he decided to visit a brothel. He told the madam that he wanted a girl for an hour, but that she had to have gonorrhoea. The madam was horrified, first that this sad, wrinkled geriatric could even get it up in the first place, and secondly because of his strange request. After arguing, the old man unzipped his fly and proudly showed her the effect of Viagra. This shut her up; she relented and went to one of her girls.

'Listen Darleen, tell the old guy outside that you've got gonorrhoea and give him a good time.'

Darleen took the old man by the hand to her room. An hour later they had made love three times. Darleen was so impressed by his performance that she felt guilty about lying to him.

'I've got a confession to make,' she told him as she was getting dressed. 'I don't really have gonorrhoea,' she admitted.

'You do now,' the old man replied.

How many Viagra users does it take to screw in a light bulb?

– One. Viagra users will screw anything.

Money was tight so Tom and Christine were forced to move in with Tom's middle-aged parents, sleeping in the lounge that had been converted into an extra bedroom. When this arrangement was discussed, Tom had no idea that his father was taking Viagra and that his parents had a very, very active sex life.

It first came to light when the young couple were prevented from getting to sleep by the creaking bedsprings upstairs – and the passionate groans of the parents.

'Come on Tom,' said Christine, getting amorous. 'Let's make love like your mum and dad.'

Tom and Christine had sex and went to sleep but were woken in less than an hour by the bed upstairs creaking again.

Christine nudged her husband. 'Come on Tom, let's do it again like your parents.'

They made love again and went to sleep.

Half an hour later they were again woken up by the bed creaking. Once again, Christine wanted Tom to make love to her – and he did.

Shortly after that Tom was awoken for the fourth time by his parent's bed creaking. This time he jumped out of bed and grabbed a broom, banged it against the ceiling shouting, 'Hey Dad, cut it out. I'm not as old as you!'

The only side effect is you'll have to make polite conversation for an hour before it kicks in ..

Newsflash!

Wall Street analysts announced today that Pfizer, the company which makes Viagra, has the fastest rising stocks in history...

An angry young man up in court
Claimed Viagra had made his dick short
The makers, he admonished
And said, 'I'm astonished
'The drug isn't as good as I thought'

Why did the Chinese politician keep taking Viagra?

– He thought it would help him in the forthcoming elections.

A man goes to his doctor and, trying not to get too embarrassed, admits that he has a sexual performance problem and needs help.

'Oh, that's not a problem anymore!' announces the proud physician. 'They've just come out with this new wonder drug, Viagra, that does the trick! You take a pill and your problems are history.'

After a brief examination the doctor gives the man a prescription and sends him on his merry way. A couple of months later, he bumps into his patient on the street.

'Doctor, Doctor!' exclaims the man excitedly, 'Thank you! Thank you! This drug is wonderful! It's an absolute miracle!'

'Well, I'm glad you think so,' says the pleased physician, 'And what does your wife think about it?'

'Wife?' asks the man, 'I haven't been home yet.'

Newsflash!

A drug that has the reverse effect of Viagra has recently been announced. Trials are already underway in the White House.

12 reasons why doctors are likely to refuse to give you Viagra

1. Because they can.
2. It costs too much.
3. They like to see a grown man cry.
4. In their 'expert opinion', you're not impotent enough.
5. You're not a fellow Freemason.
6. They don't believe you when you say you're humping for Britain in the 2000 Olympic Games.
7. They're keeping it all back for themselves.
8. You haven't got any dirt on them.
9. They fancy their chances with your missus.
10. They don't fancy you.
11. They know you live alone with an alsatian…
12. You haven't offered a big enough bribe.

How many Viagra users does it take to screw in a light bulb?

– Three. One to screw it and two to listen to him brag about how many times he did it.

What was so unusual about the medical trials for Viagra?

– The more cock-ups they had, the better.

Excitement gripped the gentleman's club when it was discovered that a 70-year-old millionaire had married a 19-year-old lingerie model. One of the members asked him how he managed to do it.

'I just did two things,' he smugly replied. 'First I told her I took Viagra. Then I told her I was 90.'

Newsflash!

Opinion is divided as to whether Viagra is responsible for the deaths of elderly men. Some scientists claim what was first seen as a cure for impotence is really just early signs of rigor mortis.

A man goes to his doctor on Friday and confides that he's just met these two busty twins who have the hots for him and they're going to spend the whole weekend at his flat.

'You've got to help me!' he pleads. 'I need something to make it hard and keep it hard for 48 hours!.' The doctor is reluctant to help but in the end he gives the man a bottle of extra strength Viagra, normally prescribed for stud horses. He tells him to swallow a handful of tablets an hour before the girls are due to arrive.

Early on the Monday morning the doctor was astonished to see the man sitting on the surgery doorstep. He looks shagged out, like death itself and whispers in a gruff voice. 'I need some Deep Heat now! I can't wait for the shops to open.'

'You can't put Deep Heat on your penis!' the doctor replied. 'You'll die from the pain!'

'It's not for my penis, Doc,' the man gasped. 'It's for my wrist. Those twins never turned up!'

How do doctors learn about Viagra?

– Through on-the-job training...

Newsflash!

Unconfirmed rumours on Wall Street have it that Bill Gates has made a tender offer for Pfizer shares. If his takeover is successful, the new company will be named Microhard.

After taking Viagra for the first time, a crusty old lord woke up to find an unaccustomed bulge in his pyjamas. He rang for his butler and, lifting the sheets, said, 'Simpson, look at this.'

'Good heavens, My Lord,' the butler responded, 'what a most magnificent specimen. Shall I go and summon Her Ladyship?'

'Good God man, no. Don't be such a bloody fool!' the lord retorted. 'Just get my plus-fours and we'll smuggle it down to London.'

A middle-aged couple had been stranded on a deserted island for many years. At first they got on well and made the best of things but then, after the husband's supply of Viagra ran out, their relationship deteriorated as both became more and more sexually frustrated.

Then one morning after a bad storm, a young man in his twenties gets washed up on the shore. The three get on very well but, after a while, it's obvious that the wife wants to be satisfied by the newcomer – who is also willing to give in to his desires. The naive husband is oblivious to the passions running high and is glad to have the second man there. For a start it means that there are three people doing 8-hour shifts in the watchtower instead of two people doing 12-hour shifts.

One day the newcomer is standing watch, looking out at the horizon for any passing ships. The husband and wife are cleaning fish which they've just caught when the newcomer shouts down, 'Hey you two! No screwing!'

'We're not screwing!' the husband shouts back. 'We're cleaning the fish.'

About ten minutes later the newcomer shouts back down at the couple, 'Hey you two! No screwing!'

The husband is perplexed but again shouts back, 'We're not screwing. We're making up a fire!'

Fifteen minutes later the newcomer shouts down, 'Hey you two! I said no screwing!'

Again the husband looks up and shouts back, 'We're not screwing. We're repairing the roof of the log cabin!'

Finally, the shift is over and the husband changes places with the young man. Before he's even halfway up the ladder to the watchtower, his wife and the young man are at it, on the beach.

Once he reaches the top the husband looks down and says to himself, 'Son of a bitch! He's right. From up here it does look like they're screwing!'

A True Viagra Fact!

Roberta Burke (63) sued her 73-year-old millionaire lover Frank Bernardo for $2 million after he left her for a younger woman in May this year. Frank decided to dump her three days after overcoming his impotence thanks to Viagra. His parting words were, 'It's time for me to be a stud again.'

Did you hear about the man who took Viagra to save his marriage but discovered he had an allergic reaction to it?

– He broke down in tears and had a lump in his throat.

Pfizer have invented a pill for elderly men which will make them sexually active. Now all they have to do is invent a pill for women so they'll find elderly men attractive.

A Viagra user named Bill
Was addicted to his special pill
His penis reached a great height
'Till it was soon out of sight
And the altitude made him quite ill

Henry – you know how you can only get an erection if I dress up like a scuba diver? Well now I've got these little pills!

A brunette was concerned that her pubic hair was turning a reddish colour. Her doctor examined her, acknowledged that she was in good heath and then asked how often she and her husband had sex. 'Twice a week?' he enquired.

'Oh, no,' she replied.

'Once a week then?'

'No. Less often than that. You see, my husband's impotent.'

'Twice a month?'

'No.'

'Once a month?'

'No.'

'Once every three months?'

'No.'

'Twice a year?'

'On average.'

'I see,' said the doctor. 'Then there's absolutely nothing to worry about. It's just rust.'

What do you call a 90-year-old man who's just made love twice in one night without Viagra?

– An ambulance

20 Top Viagra films

1. *Die Hard*
2. *The Hard Way*
3. *The Elephant Man*
4. *Doctor at Large*
5. *Deep Throat*
6. *From Here to Eternity*
7. *A Man Called Horse*
8. *Hard to Kill*
9. *Superman*
10. *Lethal Weapon*
11. *Top Gun*
12. *Giant*
13. *Hang 'Em High*
14. *Shaft*
15. *Little Big Man*
16. *The Longest Day*
17. *Moby Dick*
18. *The Long Good Friday*
19. *Anaconda*
20. *Towering Inferno*

This old man goes to the doctor for a Viagra prescription and has to undergo a full medical before the doctor declares him fit.

To his delight he passes every test. The doctor is amazed at his stamina, his low cholesterol level and the strong condition of his heart and is delighted to hand him his pills.

The man can't wait to get home and tell his wife.

'Edna, you won't believe it,' he told her. 'The doctor's told me that I can make mad, passionate love to you. He's given me Viagra and says I'm as fit as a fiddle! I feel like tearing your clothes off right here and now!'

Edna thinks for a minute and says, 'I don't know, Harry. I've heard about men having active sex at your age. I don't want it to be on my conscience if you die while we're making love. I'd feel a whole lot better if your doctor wrote a note to me saying that everything was OK. Then, once I had this, I'd be far happier about having sex with you.'

Although Harry was a little upset he understood his wife's concern and went back to his doctor the next day. He explained the situation and the doctor was happy to help him out.

'Sure I'll write you a note, Harry,' he told him. Taking his pen and his headed notepaper he began writing: Mr Harry Bloom, a patient of mine, has the heart function of a 25-year-old and can have mad, passionate sex any time that he so desires without any fear about his health, signed, Dr Jack Miller. 'Now, I'll just address it. By the way, Harry, what's your wife's first name?'

Harry paused and said, 'Doctor, just make that, "To Whom It May Concern."'

A husband was feeling particularly frisky after taking a Viagra pill so he left work early to surprise his wife. Letting himself in quietly he found her on her hands and knees, scrubbing the kitchen floor. Unable to restrain himself he lifted her dress, pulled down her knickers and took her there and then, doggy-fashion.

They made love for an hour that way and eventually the husband withdrew himself, stood up and kicked his wife in the arse.

'Is that the thanks I get for giving you so much pleasure?' she asked angrily, turning round.

'No,' he indignantly replied. 'That's for not bothering to see who it was!'

An impotent man, name of Farndon
Was just like a dead rose in the garden
At the appropriate hour
He drooped like the flower
And he just couldn't get it to harden

Despite taking Viagra, a man had a really difficult time convincing his wife to have sex with him. She was always making excuses about why she didn't feel like it.

One day he left a glass of water and two asprin on her bedside table.

'Why are these there?' she asked him. 'I don't have a headache.'

'Gotcha!' smiled her husband.

What do you call that useless, insensitive lump of fatty tissue at the end of an erect penis?

– A man

Guess who's got some Viagra!
LOTS of it??

It's not a very well-known fact but Santa Claus is, in fact, impotent. Mrs Claus finally persuaded him to see his doctor, who prescribed Viagra and they were amazed at the effect. One Christmas Eve Santa popped a couple of pills so he could give his wife a Christmas present to remember and was delivering gifts to the last few houses before returning to the North Pole.

He entered the bedroom of one little boy but was amazed to see a beautiful 19-year-old blond girl sitting up in bed.

'Santa!' she exclaimed. 'I was waiting for you!'

'Oh, I'm sorry, Miss. I was looking for little Tommy Jenkins.'

'That's my younger brother. We swapped bedrooms recently; he's down the hall.'

Santa made his excuses and went to leave but the girl, wearing the flimsiest of nighties, blocked his way.

'Don't go, Santa,' she implored. 'I just love older men.' With that she placed one of his hands on her firm breast.

'Um, I can't, I'm afraid,' said Santa awkwardly. 'I've got a few more presents to deliver.'

'Just stay here for a few minutes,' she implored, putting his other hand on her other breast.

'No really, I've, um, got to go,' said Santa, now in a sweat. 'There are toys to be delivered.'

'Please Santa. Please!' continued the girl, rubbing her hand over his crotch.

'Oh bollocks! I might as well!' replied Santa, ripping off his red tunic. 'In this state I'd never get up the bloody chimney anyway!'

Did you hear about the Viagra user who took a pill then got really worried about all the possible side-effects?

– He was scared stiff.

A busty young hooker named Marge
Would only entertain men who were large
'Viagra made me a packet
I'm proud of my racket
And the £10 per inch that I charge'

London Zoo is disappointed at the breeding success of their gorillas and decide to see what difference Viagra will make. One day the keeper hides a couple of tablets in the gorilla's feed, which he duly eats. An hour later a man and his attractive wife walk past the cage.

The woman is wearing a short, low-cut dress and as she stops to look at the great ape, he goes berserk, jumping up and down, banging on the bars, pounding his chest and grunting. He's also in an advanced state of sexual excitement.

The husband, noticing the gorilla's huge erection, urges his wife to tease the poor creature. For a laugh she blows kisses at the gorilla, wiggles her bottom, juts out her breasts, driving him wild into the bargain.

Seeing the state the ape's in, her husband suggests his wife bends over in front of the cage – which she does. He then asks her to lift up her dress and show her panties – which she does. By this time the gorilla is just about to tear the cage to pieces.

Then, as quick as a flash, the husband grabs his wife, pulls open the door to the cage and throws her in, slamming it shut behind her.

Rubbing his hands together he shouts after her, 'Now try telling him you've got a headache!'

Did you hear about the girl who said to her Viagra-taking boyfriend, 'Give me ten inches and make it hurt'?

The pill hadn't kicked in so he screwed her twice then slapped her.

The impotent bus driver goes to see his GP on the quiet, because he wants to get some Viagra, but doesn't want his wife to know. The GP prescribes him some and he goes home and makes love to his wife three times in a row. He expects her to be delighted, but instead she seems rather sad.

'What's wrong?' he asks

'I think your job is taking over your life and it's doing you in,' she replies. 'Even our sex life's like the bus service. Nothing for ages and then three come along all at once...'

A man was walking through a junkyard when he came upon an exotic-looking old bottle. He looked around and didn't see anyone, so he opened it. A genie appeared and thanked the man for letting him out. The genie said, 'For your kindness I will grant you one wish, but only one.'

The man thought for a minute and said, 'I've always dreamed of going into space and exploring the planets, but I get airsick. So I wish for a road that goes from my house and leads to all the planets in the solar system, so that I can drive up there and explore it all at my leisure.'

The genie thought for a few minutes and said, 'No, I don't think I can do that. Just think of all the work involved with the pilings needed to hold up the road and how high they would have to be to support the road as you drove out into the upper atmosphere. Think of all the tarmac that would be needed. No, that is just too much to ask.'

The man thought for a minute and then told the genie, 'There is one other thing that I'd like. I'd like my GP to prescribe me some Viagra…'

The genie considered for a few minutes and said, 'So, do you want two lanes or four?'

Is it opening time yet?

Bob had been prescribed Viagra for about a month and was back at his doctor's for a check-up after complaining about pains in his penis. The doctor ran some tests and confronted his patient with the results.

'Would you say you've enjoyed an active sex life recently?' the doctor enquired.

'I sure would,' Bob replied. 'Ever since I took that pill I've felt so randy that I've slept with a different woman every night. Some nights I even slept with three or four.'

'I see,' the doctor said gravely. 'Well that accounts for what I'm about to tell you. Do you want the good news or the bad news?'

'Oh my God!' Bob exclaimed. Bracing himself he said, 'OK Doc. I can take it. Give me the bad news first.'

'Well,' replied the doctor, 'you're suffering from an incurable strain of gonorrhoea. It's spreading at an unbelievable rate and the only way to save your life is to amputate your penis.'

Bob was stunned into silence. After a while he looked the doctor in the eye and said, 'All right. Then what's the good news?'

'You know my receptionist outside?' the doctor asked.

'Of course,' Bob said, 'the tall blonde with the huge tits.'

'That's the one,' said the doctor smiling.
'Well? Well?' asked Bob, impatiently.
The doctor smiled. 'I'm shagging her!'

10 songs all about impotence

1. 'Killing Me Softly' – Roberta Flack
2. 'After the Love Has Gone' – Earth, Wind and Fire
3. 'Ain't that a Shame' – Fats Domino
4. 'All Out of Love' – Air Supply
5. 'Don't Let It Fade Away' – Darts
6. 'Gone Too Soon' – Michael Jackson
7. 'Don't Laugh at Me' – Norman Wisdom
8. 'Can't Keep It In' – Cat Stevens
9. 'Don't Leave Me this Way' – Communards
10. 'Every Little Thing' – Jeff Lynne

Why are Viagra users better than computers?

– Given a choice, what woman would prefer a 3½-inch floppy?

A very wealthy old man was unlucky in love until he discovered Viagra. Soon after that he had three young girlfriends on the go at the same time, and was able to satisfy all three of them for hours on end.

Although he was having the time of his life, the old man was mature enough to realize that he really needed to settle down. His dilemma was who to marry. All the girls were beautiful. All of them were good in bed. In the end he decided to give them a test. He gave them each £5,000 and decided to see how they spent it.

The first girl went out and got a total makeover with the money. She bought new clothes, a new hairstyle, manicure, pedicure, the works, and told the man, 'I spent the money so I could look beautiful for you because I love you so much.'

The second girl went out and bought new golf clubs, two hand-made suits, a wide-screen TV and a stereo and gave them to the man saying, 'I bought these gifts for you with the money because I love you so much.'

The third girl took the £5,000 and invested it in the stock market, doubled her investment, returned the original £5,000 to the man and reinvested the rest saying, 'I invested the rest of the money for our future because I love you so much.'

The old man thought long and hard about how each of his girlfriends used the money he gave to them.

Finally, he decided to marry the one with the biggest tits.

Did you hear that Southampton will be sponsored by Viagra this season?

– Apparently, it's the only way they're going to stay up...

A biology lecturer at a rather stuffy English girls' school had a reputation for offending girls. A group of the more prudish ones got together and decided to walk out in protest the next time this happened.

The next week he was discussing Viagra, which had just been launched in America.

'Tests in New York', he told them, 'showed how men could sustain ten-inch erections.' As one, the girls rose from their seats and walked towards the door.

'Why are you leaving now, girls?' the lecturer asked with a leer. 'The next plane to New York doesn't leave for another three hours!'

Newsflash!

Prosecutor Kenneth Starr is reportedly investigating a rumour that the Republican Party had used Bob Dole's supply of Viagra from clinical trials to spike food deliveries to the White House.

A man asked his friend how he was getting on with Viagra. 'Well,' he replied, 'the first few days were the hardest.'

Did you hear about the absent-minded man who wasn't sure if he took Viagra or a laxative pill?

– It didn't matter because either way, he was up all night.

An elderly man is prescribed Viagra and it revolutionizes his sex drive, much to the horror and disgust of his wife. He wants to do it five times a night. He wants to do it this way, he wants to do it that way. He wants to do it in strange and unnatural ways he's never done it before.

So, not surprisingly, the strain kills him.

A few days later, his wife gets a phone call from the funeral parlour. There's a problem.

'Um…this is rather delicate,' the funeral director says, 'but your…er…husband had evidently taken so much Viagra that we can't…well we can't…that is, we can't get the coffin lid down…'

'Well, what can you do?' asks the wife, frustrated that her husband is still causing her pain even when he's dead.

'We can get a special coffin made that is about a foot deeper than standard but it will cost you an extra £150.'

'I'm not paying that,' says the wife. 'Can't you do something to solve the problem which is a little less expensive?'

The undertaker thinks for a second, then suggests, 'Well…I suppose we…we could remove his penis for you, as part of the service. Free of charge...'

'That sounds good,' says the wife. 'But I want him all there, together in his coffin, when we bury him. I don't want bits of him lying around.'

'Don't worry,' says the kindly undertaker. 'We can be very discreet. We can remove the deceased's penis and insert it in his rectum. No one will see it there when they come to view the deceased.'

Just before the funeral, the undertaker shows the wife into the chapel of rest so that she can pay her last respects to her husband, all laid out serenely in his coffin, his tell-tale bulge now removed. The undertaker closes the door of the room behind him as he leaves the wife alone with her dearly departed husband for the last time.

She bends down closer to him and then shouts in his ear, 'I told you it bloody hurts, didn't I!'

A blushing young bride from Old Wheeling
Thought a husband on Viagra so appealing
But on the honeymoon week
All the bed did was squeak
And all that she saw was the ceiling

Why don't poor people need Viagra?

– They're already hard up.

Since Viagra was invented life had never been the same at the retirement home. One of the residents, an 80-year-old man was entertaining two ninety-year-old women in his room. He managed to climb on a coffee table then dropped his dressing gown to reveal a magnificent erection. The two old dears were so shocked that one had a stroke. The other couldn't quite reach.

Newsflash!

Pfizer, the company that manufactures Viagra, announced it has set up a hot line for men who overdose on it. The way it works is, you call the number, and the operator talks you down.

A Viagra user named Sherm
Had a wonderful dick, long and firm
His ejaculation
Was the talk of the nation –
He could spell out 'I love you' in sperm

An 85-year-old man comes into the doctor's surgery looking depressed. He says, 'I think I'm impotent. I want some Viagra, please.'

The doctor sits him down and begins the standard speech he gives to senior citizens, about how, as the body ages, bodily functions slow down and it is completely normal to suffer some decrease in sexual desire, how the man shouldn't worry or become upset about it, but should just relax and things will probably be completely fine and so forth. Finally the doctor asks, 'When did you first begin to think you were impotent?'

'Three times last night and again this morning,' says the old man.

Concerned that he was prescribing too many doses of Viagra, a GP decided to get a bit more inventive about how he'd tackle middle-aged couples' flagging libido.

The next couple to come and see him were the Browns, predictably asking for Viagra. He gave them thorough physical exams, psychological exams, and various tests and then concluded, 'I'm not going to prescribe you Viagra, but I can help you to help yourselves. On your way home from the surgery, stop off at Sainsbury's and buy some grapes and some doughnuts. Go home, take off your clothes, and you, Mr Brown, roll the grapes across the floor until you hit bull's-eye in your wife's vagina. Then on hands and knees, you must crawl to her like a mighty jungle leopard and retrieve the grape using only your tongue. That will surely get you both stimulated.

'Then next, Mrs Brown, you must take the doughnuts and, from across the room, toss them at your husband until you make a ring around his penis Then like a lioness, you must crawl to him and consume the doughnut.'

The couple went home and sure enough, their sex life greatly improved.

They told their friends, Mr and Mrs Green that they should see the same doctor. The doctor greeted the Greens and then conducted the physical exams and the same battery of tests. Then he told the Greens the bad news. 'I cannot help you. I'm afraid your sex life is as good as it will ever be. I'm sorry, but I can't help.'

The Greens pleaded with him, and said, 'You helped our friends the Browns, now please, please help us!'

'Well, all right,' the doctor said. 'On your way home from the surgery, stop off at Sainsbury's and buy some apples and a packet of polos...'

Why shouldn't people with bad circulation take Viagra?

– It might give them hardened arteries.

A man went to his doctor and said, 'Doctor, I've started using Viagra but now every time I sneeze I get a massive erection.'

'I see,' the doctor replied, 'And are you taking anything for it?'

'Yes. Black pepper.'

A man went to a small pharmacy and asked if he could buy some Viagra.

The assistant apologized, saying that the shop didn't have any left. 'Have you tried Boots?' she asked.

'I want to shag my wife, not kick her head in,' the man replied.

Newsflash!

Steven Spielberg is making a film about a Viagra patient and the terrible side-effect he suffers.

It's called 'Saving Ryan's Privates'...

The man and his wife were in the marriage counsellor's office to try and resolve their sexual problems.

The counsellor asked the husband, 'Do you shrink from love-making?'

The husband replied, 'No, it's always been this size.'

Looks like it's Viagra time for Ted - he tried it on with me last night but couldn't take 'yes' for an answer

Farmer Jones's rooster was well past its prime but some crumbled-up Viagra in its corn seemed to give it a new lease of life. Although the rooster was still shagging the hens the farmer thought that maybe he did need a new stud rooster for his chicken coop. He bought a young one at the market and put it in the coop.

The cocky young rooster strutted over to the old rooster and said: 'OK, old-timer, you've had your fun. Now I'm the cock of the walk. I can handle all these hens without any of your drugs. It's time for the old to step aside and the young to take over – so take a hike!'

The old rooster thought for a minute and then said to the young rooster: 'I'll tell you what, young fellow, I'll race you round the farmhouse. Whoever wins the race gets full rights over the chicken coop.'

The young rooster laughed. 'There's no way an old'un like you can beat me! No way! But just to show I'm a sport, I'm going to give you a head start.'

The two roosters lined up at the back of the farmhouse. At the cluck of 'Go!' the old rooster took off running. After a few seconds the young rooster took off after him.

They got round the front of the farmhouse and the young rooster was only inches behind the old rooster but gaining fast.

Farmer Jones heard the squawking. Looking up he saw both birds in full flight. Grabbing his shot gun he let the young rooster have it full blast with both barrels. Blood and feathers were everywhere and the old rooster skidded to a halt, panting but otherwise all right.

'Damn!' shouted Farmer Jones as he put down his gun. That makes the third gay rooster I bought this week.'

Did you hear about the first death from an overdose of Viagra?

– A man took twelve pills and his wife died.

A Viagra user named Rick
Performed quite an unusual trick
He'd get an erection
And scorn all protection
Then balance himself on his dick

10 ways to get Viagra out of your local chemist

1. Through the skylight at 2a.m.
2. Out the back door, when no one's looking.
3. Dress up as a woman, get him to date you then threaten to spill the beans if he doesn't come across with the pills.
4. String him up, drain his blood off and then extract it by a complex chemical process.
5. Pretend to be from Trading Standards. Confiscate the entire stock under the pretext that it needs extensive testing to ensure it's genuine…
6. Tell the chemist you're from BBC Television and ask to film him outside his shop with his arms full of Viagra bottles. When he comes back out, punch him as hard as you can in the testicles and run off with as much as you can carry.
7. Train a team of delinquent rats to recognize Viagra bottles, knock them off the shelves and then roll them out of the shop as if they were walking on logs…
8. Join the fire brigade, set the chemist shop alight, then rush in with your team and 'rescue' the pills, swallowing as many as you can while ostensibly giving a succession of bottles the kiss of life…

9. Get bitten by a radioactive spider so that you can hang upside down off the ceiling, then hide up there until the shop is closed, whereupon you can help yourself.
10. Buy your own chemist shop and pig out to your heart's content

A man visited the doctor, suffering from a strange complaint.

'It's really odd, Doc,' he explained. 'The first time I make love I feel warm and comfortable all over but the second time I feel cold and shiver. Sometimes my teeth even chatter.'

The doctor gave him a full examination but couldn't find anything physically wrong with him. He asked to see his wife in private to see if she could shed any light on her husband's condition.

'He tells me that the first time he makes love to you he's warm and comfortable but the second time he's almost freezing,' the doctor reiterated.

'That doesn't surprise me,' the wife replied. 'He's so useless in bed that the first time is in July and the second time is in December.'

Two old men were sitting together on the park bench, chatting away.

'Sam?' asked the first one. 'Are you still getting sex?'

'Almost every night,' replied Sam.

'At your age – and without Viagra. I just don't believe it!' was Henry's response.

'It's true, Henry. I almost had sex on Monday night, almost on Tuesday night, almost on Wednesday night…'

Newsflash!

Gardening experts announced an alternative to staking tomato plants. Just dissolve a Viagra tablet in the water and they stand up straight and tall.

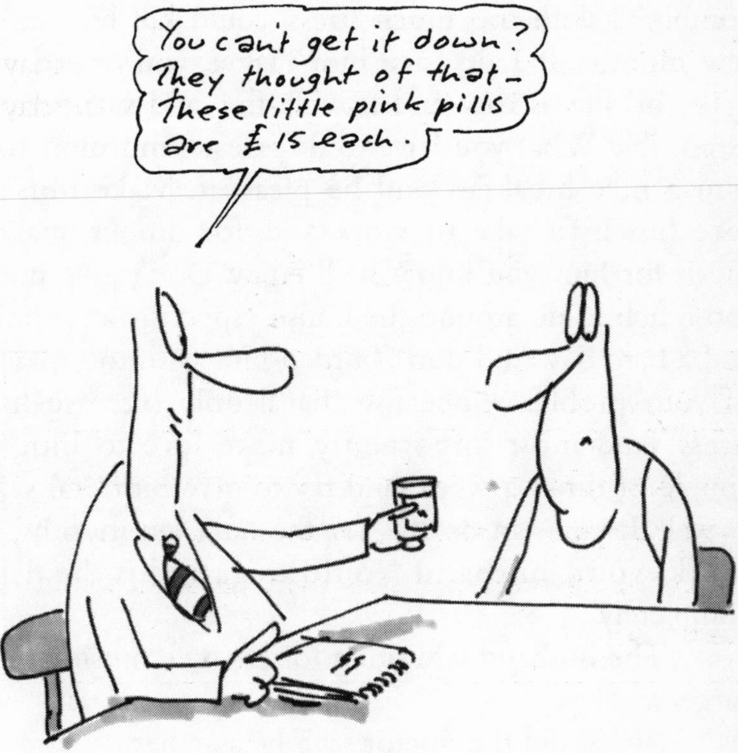
You can't get it down? They thought of that – these little pink pills are £15 each.

After years of putting up with his lousy performance in bed, a wife takes her husband to the doctor's office. After his check-up, the doctor calls her into his office and says, 'I could give your husband Viagra but only under the most controlled circumstances. Your husband is suffering from a heart condition, which, if combined with too much stress, could kill him in a few months. If I do give him Viagra, you've got to make his life as easy and trouble-free and wonderful as possible. What you have to do is, each morning, fix him a nice breakfast and be pleasant. Make him a nice lunch to take to work and, for dinner, make meals for him you know he'll enjoy. Don't give him too much to do around the house, especially after he's had a hard day. And don't burden him with too many of your problems, because that'll only increase his stress. And most importantly, make love to him a couple of times a week, and try to give him oral sex as well. If you can do this for the next ten months, I think your husband could regain his health completely.'

The husband is waiting for his wife outside the surgery.

'What did the doctor say?' he asks her.

She throws him a bottle of Viagra pills and says, 'You're gonna die.'

Pete had been impotent all his life but was too embarrassed to do anything about it. On the eve of his wedding, he finally plucked up the courage to see his doctor and explain his problem. Although sympathetic, the doctor couldn't prescribe Viagra, citing an overspend on his budget.

Pete got married anyway and everything went smoothly for the next twenty years. Their sex life wasn't very exciting, but that's because Pete always insisted on making love in the dark. After 20 years of reading articles in *Cosmopolitan* about trying new things in the bedroom, his wife planned a surprise.

One night they were making love when she suddenly reached out and turned on the bedside light.

'Oh my God!' she yelled, as she looked down between Pete's legs. There, clamped to the inside of his thigh was a banana. His wife jumped clean out of bed in shock.

'How long have you been doing that to me?' she asked.

'All our married life,' Pete confessed.

'You've got some explaining to do!' his wife shouted at him.

'Fine,' he shouts back. 'Right after you explain our three children!'

Three couples, one elderly, one middle aged and one young newlywed couple, wanted to join a very strict Christian church. The vicar told them, 'The most important part of God's ministry we preach here is, 'lead us not into temptation.' We must put His needs before our own. So, before you can join us, you must pass this test. Here is some Viagra. I want you men to take it every 24 hours for the next two weeks – but still refrain from having sex. If you can overcome that temptation, then you are strong enough to serve God's will at our church.'

The couples agreed and came back at the end of two weeks.

The vicar went to the elderly couple and asked, 'Were you able to abstain from sex for the two weeks?' The old man replied, 'No problem at all, Vicar.'

'Congratulations! Welcome to our church!' said the vicar.

The vicar went to the middle-aged couple and asked, 'Well, were you able to abstain from sex for the two weeks?' The man replied, 'The first week was not too bad. The second week I had to sleep on the couch for a couple of nights but yes, we made it.'

'Congratulations! Welcome to our church,' said the vicar.

The vicar then went to the newlywed couple and asked, 'Well, were you able to abstain from sex for two weeks?' 'Well, Vicar, we were not able to go without sex for the two weeks,' the young man replied.

'What happened?' enquired the vicar.

'My wife was reaching for a can of beans on the top shelf and dropped it. When she bent over to pick it up, I was overcome with lust. It was just too much for me. I am ashamed to say that I took advantage of her right then and there.'

'You understand, of course, this means you will not be welcome in our church,' snarled the vicar.

'That's OK,' said the young man, 'We're not welcome at Tesco anymore either.'

Newsflash!

Burger King are apparently going to be giving away free Viagra with meals. It's part of their 'home of the whopper' campaign.

Why do ugly men take Viagra?

– Wishful thinking.

Newsflash!

Pfizer are looking for more volunteers to test Viagra for side-effects. A company spokesman said, 'It's a hard job but someone's got to do it...'

A Viagra user from Kent
Had a stiffie so long that it bent
To save himself trouble
He put it in double –
And instead of him coming – he went!

Actually I dyed an aspirin blue – but the important thing is – it worked!

Why is Viagra like being robbed by a highwayman?

– It makes you stand and deliver

A man went to the chemist to pick up his first Viagra prescription and was shocked by the cost.

'£5 a pill? That's daylight robbery,' he exclaimed.

His wife, who was with him, had a different opinion, 'Oh, I don't know. £30 a year doesn't sound too bad.'

What's the biggest drawback of Viagra for men?

– Having to make conversation for an hour before the pill kicks in...

The Queen is opening a new Sexual Disorders Hospital. She's being shown round by the Hospital's chief executive when they turn round a corner. 'You don't want to go round there, Ma'am,' the chief executive says nervously. 'That's the Viagra ward.'

'Oh, I insist,' the Queen replies. 'After all, I am a Queen of the People and one has to stay in touch.'

In the first bed a man is masturbating into a bottle. 'What on earth is that chappy doing?' asks the Queen.

'Well, Ma'am,' the chief executive says, trying to retain his composure, 'that man has taken an overdose of Viagra and is suffering from a semenal fluid build-up. If he doesn't obtain sexual relief ten times a day he'll die.'

'I see,' says the Queen, nodding.

In the next bed another man is doing the same thing.

'And what is that gentleman doing?' asks the Queen.

'He's suffering from an overdose as well, Your Majesty,' says the chief executive, still very embarrassed by the whole situation.

They pass the third bed but here a patient is receiving oral sex from a beautiful nurse.

'What about him?' asks the Queen.

'Oh it's exactly the same,' replies the chief executive, 'only he's on BUPA.'

Maurice and Ida have been married for 40 years. The last twenty of which have been loveless due to Maurice's impotence. Without the benefit of Viagra to help him, he's always had a sneaking suspicion that Ida hasn't been completely faithful during their long marriage. It's on the night of their ruby anniversary that he summons enough courage to ask her.

'Ida, I was wondering,' Maurice brings himself to ask, 'what with me being impotent and you having a woman's natural needs and desires, have you ever been unfaithful to me?'

Ida takes a deep breath and replies, 'Oh Maurice, I truly love you. I wish you hadn't asked me that question...'

'Ida, please,' Maurice continues. 'I'll always love you but I must know.'

'All right then. Yes, I have been unfaithful. Maurice, But only three times.'

'Three times. That's not so bad bearing in mind my little problem. But when were they?' he asks.

'Well, Maurice, remember when you were 45 years old and you really wanted to start your own business but everyone thought you were crazy and you couldn't get funding? Didn't you ever think it was odd that, suddenly one day, the bank manager himself came over and presented you with a cheque for a loan?'

'Oh, Ida! You did that for me! I forgive you!' said Maurice. 'But what about the second time?'

'Well, Maurice, remember when Louise announced she was getting married and you were sad because we couldn't afford to give her a beautiful wedding? Well, the caterer, Mr Lipinsky, he didn't halve his estimate out of the goodness of his own heart.'

'I can't believe it Ida, that you should do such a thing for me, and for our darling daughter. I forgive you. So what about the third time?'

'Well, Maurice, remember a few years ago, when you really wanted to be president of the golf club but you were 28 votes short...'

Newsflash!

The Irish Medical Association have pooh-poohed the effectiveness of Viagra. A spokesman said, 'We've been prescribing this stuff for a week and nothing has happened! It's the worst suppository we've ever used.'

When should you take Viagra and asprin?

– When you've got a f*cking headache.

Viagra is now more valuable on the black market than heroin or cannabis, so it's hardly surprising that drug barons are now attempting to smuggle Viagra into the UK. One drug courier has swallowed a condom full of tablets and is flying into the UK. Unknown to him however, the condom has burst inside his stomach. As he passes through UK Customs he's immediately pounced on and arrested.

'What gave me away?' he asked as the Customs officers haul him off in handcuffs.

'That's easy,' one of the Customs officers replies, 'No one's that happy to see Luton Airport…'

What's the definition of 'Sod's Law'?

– Being washed up on an uninhabited desert island with a crate of Viagra.

Give me a break-
not another one
of THOSE!

Alan was a lawyer having a drink with one of his legal buddies at a bar after work. An attractive, busty woman nearby happened to hear him tell his friend that he was using Viagra. She came over, looked him straight in the eyes and said, 'I've always wanted to meet a man who takes Viagra. I'll give you £500 if you come back to my place and let me strip you naked, rub baby oil all over your body, give you the most sensuous massage ever, let you play with my tits and then let you shag me any way you want to for as long as you like.'

'I'm not sure,' said Pete, thinking about the proposition. 'What's in it for me?

Newsflash!

A new wonder drug has hit the market that's a cross between Viagra and Prozac. A spokesman for the manufacturers said, 'If you don't get a f*ck, you don't give one.'

15 things to avoid, an hour after you've taken Viagra

1. Press ups on a hard surface
2. Remembering your wife's gone away for a few days
3. Giving your mother–in–law that long–promised swimming lesson
4. Resuming your job as a department store Santa…
5. Going jogging in tight shorts
6. Operating a bacon slicer
7. Limbo dancing
8. Standing in a tightly packed queue
9. Sharing a hot tub with your granddad
10. Collecting your OBE
11. Going to a fancy dress party as Tarzan
12. Slow dancing with your granny
13. Shopping (you're almost certain to be nabbed as a suspected shoplifter)
14. Running in a baton–passing relay race
15. Wearing Lycra cycling shorts

Did you hear about the man who absentmindedly left a Viagra tablet in his shirt pocket when he sent it to the laundry?

– Now, it's too stiff to wear.

A man goes to see his doctor and explains that he's impotent and would like some Viagra. The GP gives him a full medical check, then turns to him gravely and says, 'I'm sorry, but you've got a weak heart. I can only give you thirty Viagra pills. If you take another one after that, it'll kill you for sure.'

The man walks home and finds his wife waiting for him at the front door.

'What did the doctor say?' she asks.

He explains the situation to her and she looks at him in horror. 'Oh no, only 30 more erections in your lifetime! We shouldn't waste them. We must make a list of where and when!'

'Yes,' her husband agrees, 'I thought of that. I already made the list on the way home. Trouble is, your name's not on it...'

A middle-aged couple were experiencing all kinds of marital problems, not least of which was the husband's chronic impotence and lack of any sort of sex drive. His wife begged him to go see his doctor, but he just couldn't be bothered.

In the end, the couple decided to go to see a marriage guidance counsellor. After listening to the couple's story, the counsellor suddenly jumped up, threw the wife on the floor, pulled down his trousers and pants and proceeded to make mad, passionate love to her. The husband just stared, speechless.

The counsellor looked over at the husband and told him, 'See! Your wife needs that at least twice a week!'

The husband scratched his head and replied, 'Well, I think I can get her over here on Tuesdays and Thursdays…'

Why are a 65-year-old man and Viagra like an old banger?

– They both need a hand start and you have to jump on board while they're still going.

The 90-year-old millionaire was devastated by the news that, due to his heart condition, he could not be prescribed Viagra.

'I'm ruined! Ruined!' he sobbed in the doctor's surgery. 'I'm married to the sexiest, most stunning 20-year-old in the world who's going to leave me unless I can satisfy her in bed this weekend. Not only that, but she's going to take me for half my fortune.'

The doctor took pity on him and, knowing how wealthy the patient was, told him that he might have a solution. A sonically controlled penile implant.

The doctor explained that this was still in the early stages of development but, basically, a small operation was all that was needed to insert the device in the man's penis. Just saying the word 'Beep-Beep' would give him an erection of Viagra proportions. To get rid of the erection all he needed to do was say, 'Beep.'

'Fantastic,' said the millionaire, 'operate on me now!'

'I should tell you of its disadvantages though,' added the doctor. 'The first is that it costs £125,000 and the second is that you can only use it three times.'

'That's fine!' said the patient, getting out his chequebook. 'Money's no object and all I need to do is satisfy her once this weekend.'

The operation went ahead and the millionaire came to from the anaesthetic. He lifted his sheets and said 'Beep-Beep'. Immediately, he had a huge erection. 'Beep,' he said and it receded. Satisfied that it was working he jumped in his car and ordered his chauffeur to drive him straight home. On the way a small car swerved in from of him. The chauffeur beeped the horn twice – and the old man had an erection. The small car responded with a single 'Beep,' and his erection went down.

Panicky because he only had one opportunity left, the old man asked his driver to get him home as soon as possible. Racing up the stairs to the bedroom he took his clothes off and jumped into bed next to his young bride, shouting 'Beep-Beep'. His penis had just stood to attention when his wife looked at him and asked, 'What's all this "Beep" crap?'

A Viagra user from Spain
Could make love just like a train
With vigour and power
He came every hour
Again and again and again

Two hunters who were on Viagra decided to go into the wilds for a week to go trapping. This was the first week they'd been away from their girlfriends and, since they still had the drug coursing through their systems, they were worried what would happen when they felt horny.

They were explaining this to the owner of the shop as they stocked up with food, ammunition and bait.

'These might come in useful,' said the owner, handing each man a large wooden board with a fur-lined hole in the middle of it. 'If you feel yourself getting frisky just put your dick in the hole and satisfy yourself that way.'

The two men sneered contemptuously and told the shopkeeper they wouldn't be needing them. He told them to take them anyway – they could always be used as firewood.

A week later only one of the hunters returned.

'Where's your friend?' enquired the shopkeeper.

'I shot the bastard,' the man replied. 'I caught the son of a bitch making out with my board.'

Why did you refuse to work last night?
Because with HER it is work

Why is 'It'll Be All Right On the Night' like The Viagra Testing Laboratories?

– They're both full of enormous cock-ups.

One man who certainly doesn't need Viagra appears to be Bill Clinton. In fact, one day, a White House aid came into the Oval Office to find the President wearing a pair of women's panties on his arm.

'Mr President,' he said, 'why are you wearing a pair of ladies' panties on your arm?'

'Well,' said Clinton, 'you've heard of a nicotine patch...'

Newsflash!

Recent statistics show that the demand for Viagra is now down. It is now apparent that women are not that excited about having sex with old, wrinkly men.

A man goes to his doctor and says, 'Doc, those Viagra pills are great, but they've given me this unforeseen side-effect.'

'And what's that?' asks the doctor.

'Well,' the patient confides, 'every day I wake up with a huge stiffie and give the wife a quick one. Then I go to work. I give my neighbour's wife a lift into town, and she gives me a blow job during the ride. At work, during the first coffee break, I go into the stationery storeroom and screw one of the young typists. At lunch, I take my secretary to a hotel and give her a good seeing to. During the afternoon break, I hump the personnel manageress. On the way home I give my boss's PA a lift and shag her in the back seat before dropping her off. Then, when I get home, I screw the au pair. And then at night, I poke the old lady again.'

The doctor says, 'So what's the odd side-effect?'

The man says, 'It hurts when I jerk off.'

Why is Viagra like Disneyland?

– There's a one-hour wait for a two-minute ride.

Why isn't it wise to have oral sex with a 12-inch penis?

– You might catch foot-in-mouth disease.

A Viagra user from the Coast
About his manhood, would always boast
The size of his willy
Scared his wife silly
(Now she looks like she's just seen a ghost)

Newsflash!

Scientists today warned about the new Viagra computer virus. It turns your floppy disk into a hard drive. Computer users should also beware of the Viagra supervirus; this sucks all your data off the hard drive.

What's the definition of a nymphomaniac's dilemma?

– Meeting a man who's got Viagra and VD

A couple had been married for forty years and just when they thought the passion had gone out of their love life, along came Viagra. The husband was so excited after taking his first pill that he suggested they made love in the same places they visited on their honeymoon. They jumped in the car and an hour later were driving through beautiful, secluded woods. Turning down a lane they passed a field bordered by a tall fence.

The husband turned to his wife and said, 'Dearest, do you remember how we made love right here, all those many years ago?'

His wife smile and nodded. Soon they were out of the car. The wife was leaning against the fence and they were making love like animals.

Back in the car, the man said, 'Darling, I don't remember you moving like that forty years ago – or any time since then, in fact!'

His wife replied, 'Forty years ago that fence wasn't electrified!'

Did you hear about the impotent Irishman who waited until he was 64 before asking to be prescribed Viagra?

– He'd heard that most couples had sex just before retiring.

The man was in the bathroom taking Viagra. He tried to wash it down with water but the tap came away in his hand. Then he tried to leave the bathroom but the door handle came away in his hand. For four days he was afraid to take a piss.

Newsflash!

Earlier today a van carrying Viagra skidded off the embankment and crashed into the Thames. Moments later Tower Bridge went up.

15 unexpected side-effects of Viagra

1. You lose all interest in that 1:12 scale matchstick model of the *Titanic* you've been building.
2. You bother to speak to your wife again.
3. You have to think up a new pet name for 'Mr Floppy'.
4. A total collapse in jigsaw sales
5. And Kleenex
6. Middle-aged businessmen whistling on the tube in the morning
7. Snogging on the back seats of pensioners' coach outings
8. Good-natured bosses
9. Unfinished Tom Clancy novels on countless bedside tables
10. You start wearing your teeth to bed again.
11. A huge upsurge in demand for Ralgex
12. Countless sheltered accommodation scandals
13. Your wife starts getting far more headaches.
14. Sheepish–looking pensioners hanging around the condom counter in Boots…
15. Queues the length of Gloucestershire outside surgeries

Letter to a problem page in a women's magazine:

Please help me. We used to have a normal sex life but after taking Viagra my husband has turned into a sex maniac. He takes pill after pill after pill and makes love to me as soon as I wake up, when I'm in the shower, when I'm cooking breakfast, when I'm making dinner, while we're eating dinner, when I'm watching the TV, even when I'm trying to get ready for bed. What can I do?'
From Weary of Wolverhampton.
PS Please excuse my shaky handwriting.

Well – you seem pleased to see me!.
I'm pleased to see anyone

What famous action in World War Two has an association with Viagra?

– The Battle of the Bulge

Two woman were talking about their husbands.

'Mine's not that good in bed,' the first woman admitted a bit sheepishly. 'When he does eventually come, he's very quiet.'

'That's nothing,' her friend says. 'He takes Viagra and when he climaxes, he screams at the top of his voice.'

'That must be very satisfying for you,' the first woman said, enviously.

'No. Not really. It just wakes me up.'

A Viagra patient named Rick
Could play the violin with his dick
With his humungous erection
He played a selection
From Mozart's Symphony No. 6

Newsflash!

A Viagra patient ended up in hospital today after accidentally mis-reading the instructions on a bottle of Viagra tablets: 'Screw in an anti-clockwise direction.'

A man was returning home after a date with his new girlfriend, a nurse. As he pulled up outside her house the nurse expected a goodnight kiss. What she got however, was his erect penis in her hand.

'I'm on Viagra,' he told her 'and thought you might like to give me a thorough examination.'

The girl was absolutely horrified. She slapped him round the face, leapt out of the car and stormed up to her front gate.

'I've got two words for you, you pervert,' she shouted. 'Drop dead!'

'Well I've got two words for you,' the man shrieked back. 'Let go!!!!!'

15 things you can always do if your GP won't give you Viagra

1. Jump up and down on his smug face.
2. Follow another user out of the chemists and mug them.
3. Crouch in a corner and go, 'whimper, whimper'.
4. Buy a really big car.
5. Train spotting
6. Have your wife hypnotized so she thinks a limp penis is really attractive.
7. Have yourself hypnotized so that you subconsciously believe eating a shepherd's pie will give you an erection.
8. Find a faith healer with warm hands and a big bust.
9. Carry on pretending that you've 'just had a hard day at work.'
10. Get a good job looking after an Arab Sheik's harem.
11. Become Pope.
12. Find a manufacturer of very small airships and have one constructed over your groin and then inflated.
13. Have a sex change.
14. Find an alternative way to make your penis swell – like hitting it with a claw hammer or sticking it in a bee hive.
15. Kill yourself and get it over with.

Why are doctors being criticized for their policy about prescribing Viagra?

– Some people claim they just give it out willy-nilly.

A TRUE VIAGRA FACT!

Polish medical authorities have not only approved Viagra for the Polish market, but they will also be subsidizing it! A government minister said this was to 'boost births in our homeland.'

Why did Jesus take Viagra?

– He thought he'd need it for the second coming...

What have a soft drink and a bunch of dwarfs on Viagra got in common?

– Seven Up

Newsflash!

Pfizer have just launched a Japanese version of their wonder drug, called 'Viagla'. A company spokesman said that this was inevitable given the country was the Land of the Rising Sun.

What's the difference between a woman and a computer?

– A computer can't turn a 3-inch floppy into a hard drive in a matter of seconds.

You can't get it up? Where have you been – on Mars?

A 76-year-old man got married to a 21-year-old. A few weeks later he went to see his doctor for a check-up. The doctor asked him how things were going in the relationship.

'Not bad,' the old man said 'except that I can't rely on that Viagra you gave me. Sometimes it works and sometimes it doesn't. When it does work we have great sex in the bedroom.'

'But what about when it doesn't work?' asked the inquisitive doctor.

'Well then she always wants to make love in the back seat of my car,' said the old man.

'And that hurts your back?' the doctor replied.

'That's not the problem, it's just that she insists that I drive.'

Newsflash!

Following the recent interest created by the movie, new plans are being made to raise the *Titanic.* Experts plan to pump it full of Viagra, and let nature take its course.

What was the first thing Adam said to Eve?

– 'Stand back, I don't know how big this thing gets.'

Did you hear about that 85-year-old man who tried to rape a woman before his Viagra started working. He was charged with 'assault with a dead weapon'.

Have you heard about the newly discovered Viagra Falls?

It's a new waterfall that flows upwards.

Two old men bumped into each other in a street.

'Long time no see, Joe,' said the first old man. 'Last time we met you'd just started taking Viagra. Are you getting any on the side?'

Joe sighed and said, 'I haven't had any for so long, I didn't realize they'd moved it.'

A showbiz agent hears through a friend of a friend of a man who takes Viagra and can then shag 50 women, one after the other. He meets up with him and puts forward a business proposition.

'Listen,' he tells the man enthusiastically, 'If I promote a show where you screw 50 women in a row everyone will flock and see it. I'll call you The Great Shaggo. I'll book the London Palladium and we'll charge a £20 entrance fee. We'll both be rich. What do you say?'

The man agrees to do it and posters go up to advertise the sexual prowess of The Great Shaggo. Eventually the night of the show comes round. The Palladium is packed with expectant punters. Eventually the curtain rises to see a double bed and The Great Shaggo, naked. He explains that he's already taken his pill and rings a bell for the first girl to appear. She walks on stage equally naked and they make love.

Afterwards he gives her a kiss and she walks off. The bell is rung again and the next girl walks on. The Great Shaggo lives up to his name. The crowd roar with approval every time he gets through another girl. Soon he's on number 46, then 47, then 48. After this last girl he realizes he's in difficulties and whispers to the promoter who's waiting in the wings, 'It's no good. I can't get it up again!'

'What do you mean!' the promoter whispers back. 'We promised 50 girls and you've only screwed

48. The audience will demand their money back. They'll kill me! What's gone wrong?'

'I don't know,' the performer said sheepishly, 'Everything was fine this afternoon at rehearsal.'

The man confessed to his doctor, 'Doctor, this Viagra you gave me has turned me into a sex maniac. I think about making love to women all the time. Every time I see a woman, I imagine screwing her. Whenever I meet a woman, instead of saying, "Good morning" or "Hello", I blurt out "Fancy a shag?" I'm picking up or propositioning women all the time and it works. They just can't say no. I tell you, those pills are causing me no end of trouble. I can't live a normal life anymore.'

'I see,' said the doctor. 'Tell me, how long has it been since you last had sex.'

The man thought for a few moments. '1959.'

'1959?' asked the doctor incredulously.

The man seemed puzzled then looked at his watch. 'But it's only 20.42 now…'

A old man from East Istanbul
Used Viagra every night as a rule
One time he did cry
But he soon realized why
His zip had got caught on his tool

A young woman went to confession. Upon entering the confessional she said, 'Forgive me Father, for I have sinned.'

The priest said, 'Confess your sins and be forgiven.'

The young woman said, 'Last night my husband came home with some Viagra and made mad passionate love to me – six times.'

The priest thought long and hard and then said, 'Six times? Take six lemons and squeeze them into a glass and then drink the juice.'

The young woman asked, 'Will this cleanse me of my sins?'

'No, but it will wipe that stupid smile from off your face.'

But Mr Strumpfenberg – when I said I hoped I could make it big I meant in showbusiness!

Did you know that sex with Viagra has been described as 'the most fun you can have without laughing.'

Why are vampire hunters like doctors prescribing Viagra?

– They both try and raise the dead

'I told you!' said Jim's wife. 'I told you the doctor wouldn't give you any Viagra. You'll have to carry on being useless in bed!'

Jim sighed, 'There must be some other way. Some other way to help my penis grow that doesn't involve Viagra.' He thought for a minute, then said, 'I know…I'll try rubbing it vigorously with toilet paper every day!'

'What?' his wife snorted. 'Do you think that will make your penis grow?'

'I'm not sure,' Jim said, 'but it certainly worked on your arse…'

A father and his young son go into the chemist's together. At the counter the son notices a huge variety of condoms available and asks his dad why there's so much choice.

The father replies, 'Well, you see that packet of 3? That's for when you're in school. You have 2 for Friday night and 1 for Saturday night.'

'All right, Dad,' the son continues. 'But what about that packet of 6?'

The father replies, 'Well, that's for when you're at university. You have 2 for Friday night, 2 for Saturday night, and 2 for Sunday morning.'

'OK, Dad, what about that packet of 12?'

'That's for when you're my age, Son. You have one for January, one for February, one for March...'

How do you recognize a Viagra-taker at a nudist camp?

– He's the one who can carry two cups of coffee and a dozen doughnuts at the same time.

A 90-year-old millionaire has been taking Viagra but, although he's rich and no longer impotent, he's so scrawny, toothless and ugly that he finds it really difficult to get a date. Eventually, however, one gold-digger agrees to go out with him.

The old man takes her to a nice restaurant and buys her a fancy dinner with expensive wine. Just before they leave he takes one of his tablets and washes it down with champagne. An hour later, on the way home, he pulls over to the side of the road. He puts his hand under the girl's skirt but she stops him, saying that before she has sex, she wants to know him better.

'OK,' the man replies, but how about a blow job then?'

'Yuck!' says the girl grimacing. 'I'm not putting that old thing in my mouth!'

'All right,' he says, 'How about a hand job?'

'I've never done that,' the girl says. 'What do I have to do?'

The old man can't believe she's never heard of a hand job and tries to explain it by saying, 'You remember when you were younger and you used to shake up a Coke bottle and spray your little brother with it?' She nods.

'Well, it's just like that.'

With that, the man unzips his flies and she takes hold of his erection and starts shaking it.

A few seconds later, he goes cross-eyed and his head flops back. His nose starts to run, wax blows out of his ears and he screams out in agony.

'What's wrong?!' the girl cries out.

'For Christ sake!' the man yells. 'Take your thumb off the end!'

The GP referred a rather shy man to the clinic of his local hospital for a thorough check-up before he would prescribe Viagra. The man was so embarrassed about going through the examination that he decided to have a drink to steady his nerves. And then another. And another. So that, by the time he arrived at the hospital, he was completely pissed. He went in completely the wrong entrance and ended up in the podiatrist's wing instead and weaved unsteadily over to the receptionist. Without looking up she waved him over to the examination bed and said, 'Go over there and stick it through that curtain.'

The man did so. The receptionist looked up, screamed and then yelled angrily, 'That's not a foot!'

'Oh my God,' exclaimed the man, 'you mean there's a minimum?!'

When Fred finally got himself some Viagra, he was mercilessly teased by Dave and Jim, his mates at work who boasted that they certainly didn't need any artificial help.

'Last night, I made love to my wife four times,' Dave bragged, 'and this morning she made me the most delicious cooked breakfast and told me how much she adored me.'

'Ah, last night I made love to my wife six times,' Jim responded, 'and this morning she made me a wonderful omelette and told me she could never love another man.'

When Fred remained quiet, Dave asked him smugly, 'And how many times did you make love to your wife last night?'

'Once,' he replied.

'Only once?' Dave snorted. 'And what did she say to you this morning?'

'Don't stop.'

Why is an old man without Viagra like cement?

– It takes two days to get hard.

Did you hear about the Viagra patient who attended a lecture on premature ejaculation?

– He arrived on time but found it was already over.

10 excuses for having a really small penis

1. 'I've just given blood.'
2. 'It used to be twice this size. I've just worn it down.'
3. 'I was a war baby; there was rationing.'
4. 'It's not mine. I'm on an anatomical exchange scheme with someone from China.'
5. 'I was a stunt man on *The Texas Chainsaw Massacre*.'
6. 'Who do you hang around with? Donkeys?'
7. 'I used to be a really successful gigolo. My accountant advised me to place most of my holding in a tax shelter.'
8. 'It shrank in the wash.'
9. 'We'll, you've heard of pig *heart* transplants.'
10. 'Oh my god! I've been robbed!'

What's the definition of a Viagra user with self-doubt?

– Someone who's got a mirror over the bed with the inscription, 'Objects might appear smaller than they actually are.'

The old Viagra user had just got married to his naive young bride and was explaining to her a system so he'd know if she was in the mood for sex.

'There's no need to ask me,' he told her. 'If you want to make love, just give my dick a gentle tug. If you don't want it, tug it about 55 times.'

What's the difference between 'anxiety' and 'panic'?

– 'Anxiety' is when, for the first time, you can't do it the second time.

'Panic' is when, for the second time, you can't do it the first time.

It's the world's first legal 'hard' drug
Vi

During army training, due to an administrative error, instead of receiving bromide pills to subdue their sexual desires, some of the platoon were inadvertently given Viagra. After one particularly gruelling training session, the sergeant-major decided to test the strength of his men.

'Attenshunnnn!' he bellowed, and all the men formed a perfect parade, three rows deep.

The sergeant-major slowly walked down the line thumping his baton in his hand. As he walked past one soldier he whacked him on the top of his head as hard as he could.

'Did that hurt, soldier?' he asked.

'No, sir!'

'And why was that, soldier?'

'Because I'm in the British Army, sir!'

Pleased with this response, the sergeant-major continued down the line. As he walked past another man he poked his baton into his stomach with brute force.

'Did that hurt, soldier?' he asked.

'No sir!'

'And why was that, soldier?'

'Because I'm in the British Army, sir!'

The sergeant-major nodded and continued. Near the end of the line he noticed one of the platoon had a huge erection. Smiling to himself he walked towards it and gave it the hardest wallop he could with the baton.

'Did that hurt, soldier?' he asked.

'No sir!'

'And why was that, soldier?'

'Because it belongs to the man behind me, sir!'

Why is Viagra like Karate?

– It helps you stand up for yourself

A man was so impressed with his erection after taking Viagra that he went straight down to the tattoo parlour and had 'I Love You Jennifer' tattooed in large letters all the way down his penis.

He got home and showed his wife, thinking that she'd be pleased with this tribute to her. Instead she was horrified. 'But I thought you'd like something like this,' he exclaimed.

'That's typical of you!' she replied. 'Always trying to put words in my mouth!'

A man in a food factory was taking Viagra but it made him so unbelievably horny he had this compulsion to stick his penis in the pickle slicer. This obsession was so great that he went to a psychiatrist who listened to his story intently.

'Hmmm,' he replied 'that reminds me of a similar case a while back. One of my patients had an overwhelming desire to put his hand on a hot oven. I advised him that he should go ahead and do it.'

'So what happened?' asked the factory worker.

'Well of course, he burned his hand but that cured him of the compulsion,' said the psychiatrist. 'I suggest you do the same in order to liberate yourself from this obsession.'

The man returned a week later. 'I followed your advice doctor,' he recounted, 'and stuck my penis in the pickle slicer.'

'I see. And what happened?' asked the psychiatrist.

'We both got fired.'

What do you give the Viagra patient who has everything?

– Penicillin

Newsflash!

It was announced today that there's a problem in the Pfizer laboratories. The lifts keep going up and won't come down again.

What's the difference between a tyre and 365 erections?

– One's a Goodyear and the other's an absolutely brilliant year.

A man comes home and says to his wife, 'I've got the Viagra, honey!' Pack your bags!'

'Where are we going?' his wife asks. 'A second honeymoon in Paris? A romantic weekend away in Venice? A luxury cruise?'

'No, you don't understand,' her husband replies. 'Pack your bags…'

'I'm losing my sex drive,' admitted the old man to his doctor.

'That's understandable at your age,' said the doctor. 'What you need is Viagra. Take one of these pills before you go to bed and you'll be as right as rain.'

'But how often will I be able to make love?' asked the old man.

'Well,' the doctor said, consulting his patient notes, 'you're pretty fit so I would think that twenty times a month would be fine.'

The old man took the pills and thanked him. When he got home he proudly announced to his wife that he could now make love twenty times a month. She looked at him over her bifocals and said, 'That's great, dear. Put me down for two.'

Newsflash!

Instructions on a bottle of Viagra:

Swallow immediately. Do not chew or your tongue will harden.

This is the first time I can't do it the second time
I wouldn't worry till it's the second time you can't do it the first time

50 other ways to use Viagra

1. A general could use it to raise morale.
2. An architect could use it to erect a building.
3. A coward could use it to stiffen his resolve.
4. A businessman could use it to raise profits.
5. A performer could use it to rise to the occasion.
6. Another performer could use it to be a hard act to follow.
7. A third performer could use it to make the big time.
8. A fourth performer could use it to get a standing ovation.
9. A negotiator could use it to drive a hard bargain.
10. A libertarian could use it to stand up for his rights.
11. A squaddie could use it to stand to attention.
12. A boss could use it to give an employee a stiff talking to.
13. An alcoholic could use it to enjoy a stiff one.
14. A gay couple could use it to become firm friends.
15. An exhibitionist could use it to stand out from the crowd.
16. An employee could use it to get a raise.
17. A tenant could use it to extend his lease.
18. A manic depressive could use it to avoid a downer.

19. A politician could use it for another cock-up.
20. A convict could use it to serve hard time.
21. A crook could use it to be Mr Big.
22. An arrogant man could use it to be cocksure.
23. Avis could use it to try harder.
24. A vampire hunter could use it to raise the dead.
25. A highwayman could use it to stand and deliver.
26. A thrusting young executive could use it to ensure he's up and coming with the firm.
27. A procrastinator could use it to ensure things remain up in the air.
28. A Chancellor of the Exchequer could use it to raise taxes.
29. An entrepreneur could use it to raise some money.
30. A gigolo could use it to ensure they're up to the job.
31. A romeo could use it to make himself hard to resist.
32. A journalist could use it to get hard news.
33. A Foreign Secretary could use it to create a firm foreign policy.
34. A judge could use it to impose a stiff sentence.
35. A mountaineer could use it to get a firm grip.
36. A backbench MP could use it to raise a question in Parliament.
37. A crossword puzzle writer could use it to give hard clues.

38. A builder could use it to help with an extension.
39. A construction worker could use it to protect himself with a hard helmet.
40. A comedian could use it to raise a laugh.
41. A self-critical man could use it to be hard on himself.
42. Wellington could use it to become the 'Iron Duke'.
43. The accused could use it to come up before the judge.
44. A thirsty man could use it to get 7–Up.
45. An optimist could use it to prove that things are looking up.
46. A critic could use it to be hard to please.
47. A banker could use it for a standing order.
48. A sailor could use it to raise anchor.
49. Charles Dickens could use it to write *Hard Times*.
50. A football supporter could use it to come 'up for the cup.'

Have you heard about new Viagra-DeLuxe?

– Apparently it gives you more bangs for your buck.

Three really old men were sitting on a park bench when a reporter came up to them. 'I'm researching an article on longevity and wonder if you three would be willing to tell me your secret of long life.'

The three old men nodded in agreement. The first old man said, 'I never drank alcohol, I never smoked tobacco and I have been married to the same woman for 75 years.'

'Wow, that's really remarkable!' said the reporter. 'And how old are you?' he asked the man. 'I'm 97,' came the reply.

The second man also gave his explanation. 'I drank on occasion, I smoked in moderation and I dated a bit.'

'And how old are you?' asked the reporter. 'I'm 91,' said the second old man.

Finally, the reporter approached the third old man and asked his secret of a long life. The old man replied, 'Viagra. I take three pills a night and shag everything in sight from sunset to sunrise.'

'Wow!' said the reporter. 'And how old are you?'

'Twenty-nine,' replied the man.

'Darling. I so sorry. It's never happened to me before.'

'What a limp excuse.'

What do you call the people you meet at a Viagra clinic?

– Firm friends

Jerry thought it couldn't get any better. He was on Viagra, getting erections on demand, dating hundreds of women and having the most fabulous sex life ever. One day, though, he just collapsed and was diagnosed by his doctor as suffering from nervous exhaustion.

'The only way you'll get your health back,' the doctor warned him, 'is to abstain from love-making.'

'Give up sex?' Jerry gasped. 'You're joking!'

'There's no need to give up completely from day one,' advised the doctor. 'You could taper off gradually.'

'And how do you expect me to do that?' asked Jerry.

'Get married.'

You look a bit past it but I like your friend

A man who's been prescribed Viagra goes back to his doctor about a week later complaining about two side-effects. Firstly, the pill has made his penis grow by four inches – but it's also left him with a terrible stammer.

The doctor concludes that the only way to cure the stammer is to chop off four inches – this can be done by a relatively minor operation that won't have any long-term effects.

The patient agrees and the operation is a success. His penis is its original size and the stammer has gone. The man returns, though, a few days later.

'Doc, I want you to replace that section of my penis that you cut out. My wife's decided that she doesn't mind the stammer but really misses those extra four inches.'

To this request, the doctor replies, 'I-I-I'm a-a-afraid t-t-that I-I-I c-c-can't!'

Why is a man taking Viagra like a snowstorm?

– You don't know when he's coming, how many inches you'll get – or how long it'll last.

Albert was 75. He'd just discovered Viagra and had fallen in love with, and got engaged to, a sexy 25-year-old who was more than happy with his performance in bed.

His 80-year-old friend Mortimer, however, was deeply worried about the arrangement.

'At your stage in life,' he offered, 'it might be fatal.'

Albert just shrugged philosophically. 'If she dies, she dies.'

Have you heard about the new Viagra cocktail?

– The Hard-Up Wallbanger

Two friends were sitting on a bridge fishing and soon both needed a pee. Wanting to impress his mate, the first man took a leak over the side and said, 'Wow! This water's freezing.'

'Yep,' said his friend, not wishing to be outdone, 'and deep.'

What's the first sign you might need Viagra?

– When you've been in bed with a woman all night and the dawn comes before you do.

Charlie was so obsessed by golf that he spent every spare hour practising or playing. By the time he got to bed he was too tired to make love. A friend at the golf club mentioned that he should try Viagra. 'It'll make you stiffer than a number 3 iron,' he advised.

Charlie took his first pill and was amazed by the transformation that came over him – and so was his wife. They made love for twenty minutes before Charlie rolled off to go to sleep. His wife, however, shook him about ten minutes later for another session. They shagged for another twenty minutes before Charlie rolled off again to go to sleep. Ten minutes later the same thing happened. His wife woke him up and they screwed for the third time.

After the fifth time, Charlie could stand it no more.

'There's one thing I need to know, honey,' he asked.

'What's that, stud?' answered his wife.

'What's the par for this hole?'

The day the cruise liner went down, John thought all his Christmases had come at once. He found himself shipwrecked on a desert island with six busty, beautiful girls and a whole crate of Viagra from the ship's pharmacy.

The women soon reached an arrangement where they'd each have sex with John a different night of the week and he would have Sunday off to recover.

This worked out fine but after a few months, even with the Viagra, John found he was literally shagged out, and really looking forward to his day of rest. He wished there was another man who could share the love-making duties.

One day his prayers were answered. He was fishing when he saw a life-raft bobbing up and down in the distance, drifting towards him on the tide. As it came nearer he swam out to meet it. Tired, but alive, was another man. John hugged him and said how happy he was to meet him.

'You won't believe how happy I am to see you!' he cried

The other survivor looked him up and down and said, 'Me too, gorgeous!'

'Bollocks,' groaned John. 'There go my Sundays!'

What do you get when you combine Viagra with shoe polish?

– Something that will make you rise and shine.

The Viagra user had such a large erection that none of his normal condoms would fit. He went to the chemist to explain his predicament and the sales girl asked him to follow her into a back room.

She lifted up her skirt, dropped her panties and asked him to enter her. This he did and after a few minutes she told him to take his dick out.

'Size XXXL sir. How many do you need?' The man bought two dozen and on his way home bumped into a friend. After hearing about his experience, his friend rushed straight round to the same chemist and explained that he didn't know his size.

'This way, sir,' the salesgirl said, dropping her panties once more.

After they'd finished the girl said, 'That'll be XL. How many do you want?'

'None,' said the man smiling. 'I just came in for a fitting.'

Another Viagra patient had the same dilemma. What size condoms would he need due to his king-size erections? The girl at the chemist told him that there was a fence behind the shop with three knotholes in it labelled A, B and C. If he could fit his penis in one of the knotholes comfortably and told her the letter, she would get him the appropriate size of condoms.

It was no trouble for the man to get an erection and he gingerly inserted it into knot hole A. This was a bit on the tight size, but still pleasurable. Withdrawing it, he inserted his penis in knothole B. This was tight, though not as tight as knot hole A so he could move it in and out without much trouble. Knothole C, however was just right. He could fit his penis in, and move it back and forth until he climaxed.

He went back inside the shop and the assistant asked how he got on.

'F*ck the condoms!' he answered. 'Just give me two yards of that fencing.'

Did you hear about the flasher who changed his mind about retiring?

– He decided to stick it out another year.

A TRUE VIAGRA FACT!

Jean-Louis Galland, a restaurant owner in Thonon-les-Bains, eastern France, was forced to remove a sauce containing Viagra from his menu after a visit from government officials concerned that he was dispensing the anti-impotence drug without a licence. His Beef Piccata in Viagra Sauce Infused with Fig Vinegar and Herbs was a particular favourite of his customers, especially, according to M. Galland, 'the granddads and their wives'.

What are a woman's three biggest lies?

a) You're the best.
b) You're the biggest.
c) Of course you don't need Viagra.

The bad news is the viagra proved too much for your husband's heart. The good news is his willie will be with us for another week

Newsflash!

The makers of Viagra were today served with a law suit by a man who claimed that the drug made his penis 24 inches long and unusable. When asked for a comment, a spokesman said, 'It would never stand up in court' and added, 'besides, there's no way on earth any jury would swallow that.'

A Viagra patient came running into his doctor's surgery and yelled, 'Doctor, you've got to help me! I've got this weird side-effect. I keep seeing pink-striped crocodiles!'

The doctor is astounded. He says. 'I don't think it's the Viagra. Have you seen a psychiatrist?'

'No,' says the patient, 'only pink-striped crocodiles…'

This under-endowed man was walking through a Moroccan marketplace when he accidentally kicked an old brass lamp that was lying on the floor. He picked it up, and for a joke, gave it a rub. To his amazement, a genie appeared.

'I am the genie from the lamp and I have the power to grant you three wishes,' the genie boomed.

'OK,' said the man, hardly able to contain his delight. 'I want to be well hung!'

'Your wish is my command, oh Master!' said the genie. There was a puff of smoke and the man found himself being lead to the gallows.

'No! No!' cried the man. 'That's not what I meant! I want to have a massive pecker!'

'Your wish is my command, oh Master!' said the genie. There was a puff of smoke and the man found himself staring at a 16-foot-tall woodpecker.

'No! No!' cried the man 'you've got it all wrong! I want a penis that touches the ground!'

'Your wish is my command, oh Master!' said the genie. There was a puff of smoke and the man found himself without any legs.

Did you hear about the heart patient who was accidentally prescribed Viagra?

– He took a turn for the nurse…

'Doctor,' said old Joe, 'ever since you gave me that Viagra, my wooden leg keeps giving me the most terrible pain!'

'Don't be ridiculous,' his doctor sneered. 'How can Viagra be responsible for that?'

Old Joe sighed. 'Every time I try it on with the missus, she hits me over the head with it…'

A Viagra user from Nantucket
Had a dick so long, he could suck it
As he wiped down his chin
He said with a grin
*If my ear was a snatch I would f*ck it!*

A wife asked her husband, 'why are you walking like a crab?'

The husband replied, 'It's the Viagra. It's having side-effects…'

How do you know when your Viagra's not working?

– When she says, 'Is it in yet?'

Despite the Viagra, John just couldn't get it up, so a sex therapist counselled him in other methods of love-making. A few months into his treatment, he broke some astounding news, 'My wife and I aren't having intercourse, but she's pregnant. Is it possible she can get pregnant through manual or oral stimulation?'

The sex therapist thought long and hard and then said, 'I think what we've got here is what we in the medical profession call a 'grudge pregnancy'.

'What's that?' John asked.

'Someone had it in for you.'

An old man is sitting in a pub, having just taken his first Viagra. He's particularly horny, a feeling he hasn't had since before decimalization, and is desperate to try out his newfound virility. He approaches a pretty girl he sees in the corner and says, 'If I give you £20 will you let me make love to you?'

The girl shouts out, 'Get away from me, you dirty old man.'

But he won't take no for an answer. 'Look, I'll give you £50 for sex.'

'No! Just go away or I'll call the police!' she exclaims.

'All right then, how about £200 then?'

The girl pauses to think about his offer but still declines.

'Look, I'm desperate for a shag. £500. Please!'

This makes the girl ponder. £500 is a lot for one shag. The man's so old that there's no fear of her getting pregnant and he's not that bad looking…

'Well, OK then. But just one shag. And nothing pervy either!'

They go off to her house and are soon making love on her bed, the Viagra really working.

'OH MY GOD! OH MY GOD! OH MY GOD! OH MY GOD!' he cries out as he pumps away.

Their rhythm gets faster and faster and he shouts even louder, 'OH MY GOD! OH MY GOD! OH MY GOD! OH MY GOD!' He's almost ready to come and still he screams, 'OH MY GOD! OH MY GOD! OH MY GOD! OH MY GOD!.'

The girl's curiosity gets the better of her and in the middle of their lovemaking she asks why he's shouting out like this. He tells her 'OH MY GOD! OH MY GOD! OH MY GOD! OH MY GOD...where on earth am I going to get £500 from...'

The anxious wife arrived at the reception of her local hospital, 'I'm looking for my husband, Bill Smith. I hear he was rushed here after taking a massive overdose of Viagra. Where is he? Can I see him?'

The receptionist checked her notes, 'Bill Smith? Massive Viagra overdose? Go ahead, Mrs Smith. You'll find him in wards 7,8, 9 and 10...'

'Oh God!' cried the patient. 'Doctor, help me! Ever since you've put me on the Viagra I've been at it like a rabbit and I think my eyesight's going!'

'Too right it is,' came a voice. 'This is a chip shop. The surgery's next door.'

An elderly man came bursting into his doctor's surgery. 'You gave me some Viagra and now my wife's pregnant!' he yelled.

'Congratulations,' said his doctor.

'No, it's terrible news. The last thing we wanted was a child at our age.'

'Then why weren't you taking any precautions?' the doctor asked.

'I didn't think we had to,' the man replied. 'It says "child-proof" on the bottle...'

'Doctor, the Viagra is working on me like a dream,' said the patient. 'But the problem's with my wife now. Every time I get frisky in bed, she jumps out and says she'll have none of that!'

The doctor thought for a moment, then pulled a small box out from his desk drawer and said, 'After you've gone to bed, sprinkle the contents of this box on the floor around your bed.'

The patient looked puzzled, 'Is it some kind of aromatherapy aphrodisiac?'

'No,' said the doctor. 'It's a packet of drawing pins...'

I'm sorry - my brain doesn't seem to be functioning since I took that Viagra
That's ok - it probably means the other thing is

A couple make an appointment with a sex therapist.

'And what seems to be the problem?' he asks them.

'Well,' the man says, 'I think I might be impotent and need Viagra. But I want you to make sure. Can you watch us make love, please?'

The therapist thinks this request is a bit odd but he agrees and they have sex on the consulting-room floor.

As they're getting dressed, the therapist says, 'Well, there doesn't seem to be any problem there,' and charges them £50 for his time.

A week later they come back and the man is more concerned about his virility. 'Please can you watch us make love again. I really value your opinion.'

So the couple have sex in front of him and again the therapist tells the man that he seems to be getting on fine – and that there's nothing to worry about. Again, he charges them £50 for his time and they leave.

This continues for several more weeks and eventually the therapist gets fed up.

'Look!' he tells them. 'I've watched you make love week after week after week. I'm an expert in these matters so please believe me when I tell you that you don't need Viagra!'

'I know,' the man says.

'What? But why on earth have you kept on coming back here?' the therapist asks.

'That's simple. We're having a torrid affair. I'm married so we can't make love at my house. She's married so we can't make love at her house. We live in a small town so we can't go to a hotel there. In the city the cheapest hotel room is £175 a night. If we come to you we only get charged £50 – and I can claim £20 of your fees back from BUPA.'

Barry came home with some Viagra. His wife was so overcome that she threw herself on the couch and cried, 'Barry – take me some place that I've never been before!'

So he took her to the kitchen.

'My husband's no good,' the woman told her friend.

'But you told me only last week that he was a model husband.'

'He's a model husband all right – but not a working model.'

The doctor looks up in surprise as a familiar face appears at his surgery door. 'Didn't the Viagra help?' he asks.

'Oh sure, we're making love again,' says his patient, 'but there's another problem now.'

'What's that?' asks his doctor.

'My wife is moaning too much while we're making love.'

'But that's good, isn't it?

'No – she keeps moaning about money and holidays and a new car...'

A man goes to see his GP and complains that since he became impotent he and his wife have drifted apart – to the point where they no longer sleep together. The doctor prescribes him Viagra and asks him to return in a month.

A month goes by, and the man returns.

'Are you sleeping with your wife now?' the doctor asks.

'No,' says the man as his face breaks out in a broad grin. 'No. Not a wink...'

A Viagra user from Brent
Had a penis of such an extent
It could not be supported
So his love life was thwarted
And now it is terribly bent

A Viagra user is making love to his girlfriend for the fourth time on the trot and is beginning to get sore. He doesn't want to admit this so he continues humping away. He climaxes and just when he thinks he's going to get a break his girlfriend tells him she wants more.

They make love again. And again. By this time his penis is beginning to really hurt.

After the sixth time, he tells his girlfriend that he's going to get a drink of water.

In the kitchen however, he opens the fridge and pours a half pint of cold milk into a jug, and then dunks his penis in it to cool it down; the relief is unimaginable. Just then, however, his girlfriend walks into the room and sees what he's doing.

'Aha!' she says. 'So that's how you load it.'

Nick is engaged to a beautiful girl from a religious family, who wants to save herself for her wedding night. Well Nick, who's on Viagra, is as horny as hell and can't wait for this. He decides to sow his wild oats, shagging everything in sight in the two months before his wedding.

A few days before the big day he goes to see his doctor. Endless screwing has made his penis so twisted and bent that it won't function properly.

'You and that drug have overdone it, my lad,' the doctor tells him. 'You need to rest it before your wedding night or it won't be any use to anyone. All I can do is put it in splints.'

The wedding goes off to plan and Nick and his new bride are in the honeymoon suite undressing. His wife strips off and very coyly, points between her legs and says, 'Darling, look. This has never been touched by another man.'

Nick pulls his pants down to reveal his penis in splints, saying, 'Darling, look. It's still in its original crate.'

Have you heard about the new book that explains Viagra to children?

– It's a pop-up book.

On their first night together, the newlywed couple get ready for bed. The bride comes into the bedroom just wearing a bathrobe. Her delighted husband says, 'Dearest, now that we are married, you can open your robe.'

She does so and he gasps. 'My God! My God! You're so beautiful. Let me take your photograph.'

'Why do you want to do that?' she asks, flattered.

'So I can carry it in my pocket, next to my heart for evermore.'

With that, she smiles and he takes her picture.

'Darling,' she says to her new husband. 'Now that we are married you too can take off your robe.'

So the man loosens the belt and opens his robe, at which point his wife exclaims, 'My God! My God! Let me take your photograph.'

The man smiles at her lovingly and asks, 'Are you going to keep it next to your heart?'

'No,' she shouts 'I'm going to get it enlarged!'

Newsflash!

Scientists have discovered a safer alternative to Viagra. Just watch late-night baseball on Channel 5. That way you get bored stiff.

10 things men never, ever want to hear in the bedroom

1. Is it in?
2. Don't worry. It happens to lots of men.
3. You're not as good as your brother.
4. You're not as good as your sister.
5. Doesn't it get any bigger?
6. Oh my god! My husband's home early from SAS training!
7. I'm not laughing at that. I was thinking about this joke I heard the other day. Honest!
8. Have you heard ofViagra?
9. This is Kevin. I've always wondered what it would be like watching two men…
10. This is Rex…